AN ILLUSTRATED GUIDE TO
NATO
FIGHTERS
AND ATTACK AIRCRAFT

a Salamander book

Published by Arco Publishing, Inc.
NEW YORK

AN ILLUSTRATED GUIDE TO
NATO
FIGHTERS
AND ATTACK AIRCRAFT

Bill Gunston

A Salamander Book

Published by
Arco Publishing, Inc.,
215 Park Avenue South,
New York,
N.Y. 10003,
United States of America.

© 1983 by Salamander Books Ltd.,
27 Old Gloucester Street,
London WC1N 3AF,
United Kingdom.

This book may not be sold outside
the USA and Canada.

All correspondence concerning the
content of this volume should be
addressed to Salamander Books Ltd.

ISBN 0 668 05823 4

Contents

Aircraft are arranged in alphabetical order of manufacturers' names.

Credits

Author: Bill Gunston, former Technical Editor of *Flight International*, Assistant Compiler of *Jane's All the World's Aircraft*.

Editor: Ray Bonds
Designer: Philip Gorton

Color drawings: © Pilot Press Ltd.; and by Mike Trim and Tudor Art Studios Ltd., © Salamander Books Ltd.

Map and markings: Jerry Scutts/ Alan Hollingbery; and TIGA, © Salamander Books Ltd.

Photographs: The publishers wish to thank the aircraft manufacturers, air forces and other international government archives, and private individuals who supplied photographs for this book.

Filmset by Modern Text Typesetting Ltd.

Color reproduction by Rodney Howe Ltd.

Printed in Belgium by Henri Proost et Cie.

Introduction

THIS BOOK examines the aircraft which defend NATO's 600 million people, but not in the usual way, by studying how the aircraft were designed and developed; rather by relating them to the tasks they have to do, and the squadrons which use them.

The North Atlantic Treaty was signed, despite intense Soviet pressure, on April 4, 1949. The pressure was directed mainly at the Europeans among the original signatories, who were Belgium, Canada, Denmark, France, Iceland, Italy, Luxembourg, the Netherlands, Norway, Portugal, the UK and the USA. Greece and Turkey joined the alliance in 1952, and Federal Germany in 1955; in March 1966 France withdrew from the military alliance (while remaining politically and economically a member) and Spain became a full member in May 1982.

Throughout its life NATO has suffered greatly from the fact that it exists to protect countries which are completely free democracies. To any builder of military forces it is much easier to have an organization like the Warsaw Pact (which dates from 1955). Here there is only inhibited discussion, and certainly no argument with the Soviet Union; decisions are taken centrally and quickly, and the result is a continuing avalanche of weapons which are all modern, effective, standardized and produced at the lowest cost. NATO's position is different, even in such a high-cost, technologically difficult field as combat aircraft. Democratic people vociferously maintain their independence.

The past 30 years have repeatedly monstrated how difficult it is in a free society to get an efficient collaborative programme to achieve a standard product. The most common way has been for all the supposed junior partners in NATO to buy American, or participate in a multinational manufacturing programme run by the Americans for a US product, such as the F-104 or

F-16. Further US products which have been the subject of major NATO collaborative efforts include the E-3A (AWACS), Mk 44 air-launched torpedo, Bullpup ASM, Hawk SAM, Sea Sparrow naval SAM, and Sidewinder and AMRAAM AAMS. Most of the European collaborative efforts have either foundered, or sold to only a few (as in the case of Aeritalia G91, Atlantic, Jaguar and Transall). The Tornado, though not American, stands out as an almost unique example of a programme sufficiently large, and well-managed, to result in a really competitive product which will undoubtedly find wider acceptance.

One of the stumbling blocks is that the USA, incomparably the dominant NATO power in industrial and political influence, is psychologically handicapped in multinational programmes. Such a programme based on a US product is easy to understand. A programme based on a "foreign" product is seen

Above: The Tornado F.2 is the supreme example of a modern NATO weapon system.

primarily as competition. Even Tornado, which has never had any US counterpart other than the older and less-efficient F-111, had to survive a decade of American (and French) industrial and political history. It may be that, spearheaded by the bold and unilateral decision of the US Marine Corps to buy the Harrier, the much-vaunted "two-way street" in arms across the Atlantic may eventually take on some degree of realism.

Of course, there are examples of NATO military hardware which, by their very nature, were forced to be single integrated systems created on a collaborative basis. By far the largest in physical terms is NADGE (NATO air-defence ground environment), the single giant system of radars, computers, displays and communications which stretches in a 2,000-mile (3,200km) curve from northern Norway round Federal Germany and across the Mediterranean to Turkey's eastern frontier. Yet even here the superb

grand design was flawed in the execution by nationalistic horse-trading, nationalistic technical weaknesses and other snags including a total inability to predict future rates of inflation. And, since NADGE was completed in the early 1970s, individual nations have added their own local bits, or even (in the case of Greece/Turkey in the summer of 1974) withdrawn their vital NADGE stations from the chain while they indulged in a fratricidal war.

Greece and Turkey were for both political and economic reasons two of the crucial nations when NATO was formed. They were the most in need of economic aid, and they were the most directly threatened by the Soviet Union. Not much has changed, and after 31 years in the alliance Greece remains a fragile member. Italy has a large population which habitually votes ▶

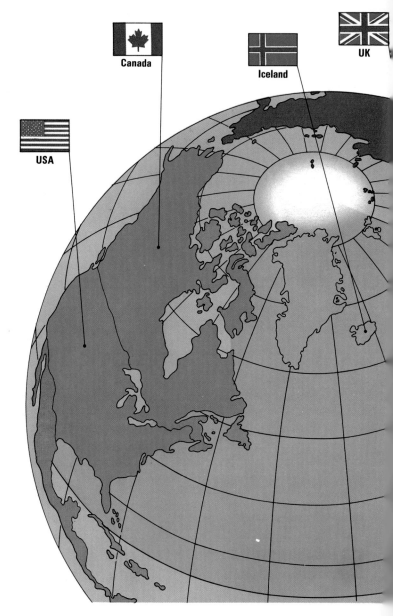

USA

Canada

Iceland

UK

▶ Communist, and it is not long since Portugal underwent a leftist revolution that was led by the armed forces, notably the air force. Next door, Spain fears a coup by an army that is equally far to the right.

All these are natural problems of a free society. They make NATO's planning a thousand times more difficult. They are also what NATO exists to protect.

The NATO command structure

For 34 years NATO's thinking has been polarized around a military assault from the Soviet Bloc directed at Western Europe. This scenario may be erroneous, but all other theatres have been regarded as strategically secondary or less likely to be the scene of conflict. Thus, though North America still has

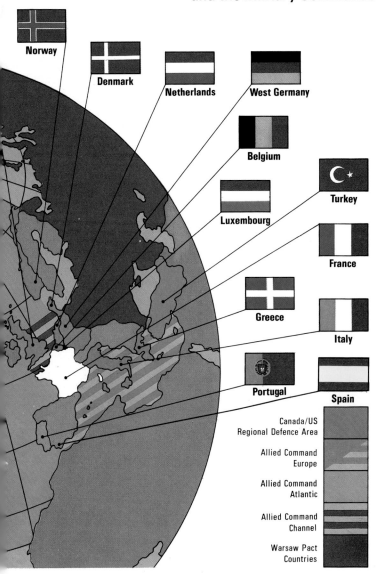

Norway

Denmark

Netherlands

West Germany

Belgium

Turkey

Luxembourg

France

Greece

Italy

Portugal

Spain

Canada/US Regional Defence Area

Allied Command Europe

Allied Command Atlantic

Allied Command Channel

Warsaw Pact Countries

powerful defences, for eventualities studied by the Canada/USA Regional Planning Group (which meets alternately in Washington and Ottawa), the only kind of attack on that vast territory that appears feasible is a nuclear assault by ICBMs and SLBMs.

This leaves three other NATO commands, each covering a particular geographical area, all of which would certainly be directly involved in any future European conflict. These are Allied Command Europe (ACE), Allied Command Atlantic (ACLANT) and Allied Command Channel (ACCHAN).

ACE is the largest and, it is assumed, most immediately threatened of these organizations. Its commander is called Saceur (Supreme Allied Commander, ▶

9

NATO Military Structure

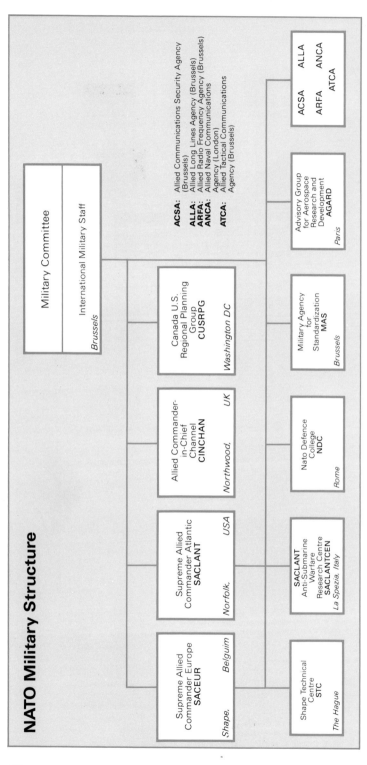

Military Committee

International Military Staff

Brussels

Supreme Allied Commander Europe SACEUR
Shape, Belgium

Supreme Allied Commander Atlantic SACLANT
Norfolk, USA

Allied Commander-in-Chief Channel CINCHAN
Northwood, UK

Canada U.S. Regional Planning Group CUSRPG
Washington DC

Shape Technical Centre STC
The Hague

SACLANT Anti-Submarine Warfare Research Centre SACLANTCEN
La Spezia, Italy

Nato Defence College NDC
Rome

Military Agency for Standardization MAS
Brussels

Advisory Group for Aerospace Research and Development AGARD
Paris

ACSA   ALLA   ANCA
ARFA   ATCA

ACSA: Allied Communications Security Agency (Brussels)
ALLA: Allied Long Lines Agency (Brussels)
ARFA: Allied Radio Frequency Agency (Brussels)
ANCA: Allied Naval Communications Agency (London)
ATCA: Allied Tactical Communications Agency (Brussels)

Allied Command Europe

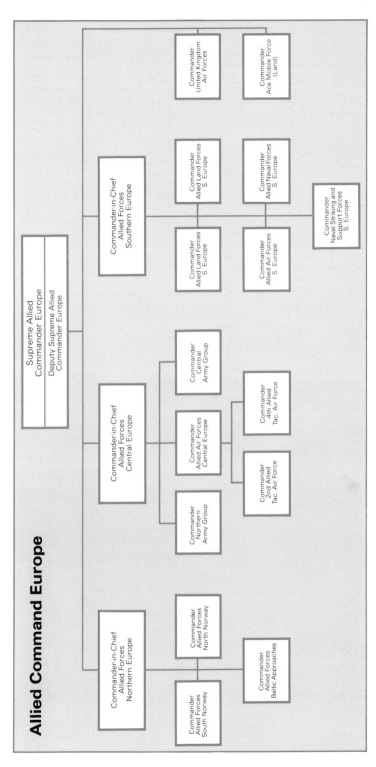

Supreme Allied Commander Europe
Deputy Supreme Allied Commander Europe

Commander-in-Chief Allied Forces Northern Europe

Commander Allied Forces South Norway

Commander Allied Forces North Norway

Commander Allied Forces Baltic Approaches

Commander-in-Chief Allied Forces Central Europe

Commander Northern Army Group

Commander Allied Air Forces Central Europe

Commander Central Army Group

Commander 2nd Allied Tac. Air Force

Commander 4th Allied Tac. Air Force

Commander-in-Chief Allied Forces Southern Europe

Commander Allied Land Forces S. Europe

Commander Allied Land Forces S. Europe

Commander Allied Naval Forces S. Europe

Commander Allied Air Forces S. Europe

Commander Naval Striking and Support Forces S. Europe

Commander United Kingdom Air Forces

Commander Ace Mobile Force (Land)

Europe), and his HQ is at Shape (Supreme Headquarters, Allied Powers Europe), which is at Casteau, near Mons, Belgium. Commands subordinate to Saceur are: Allied Forces Northern Europe, Kolsoas, Norway; Allied Forces Central Europe, Brunssum, Netherlands; Allied Forces Southern Europe, Naples, Italy; the UK Air Forces Command, High Wycombe, England; and the AMF (ACE Mobile Force), Seckenheim, Germany.

ACLANT is responsible for the largest geographical area. Its commander is Saclant, and his HQ is at Norfolk, Virginia, USA. His subordinate commands are: Western Atlantic, Norfolk; Eastern Atlantic, Northwood, England; Iberian Atlantic, Lisbon, Portugal; and three naval commands including Striking Fleet Atlantic which includes powerful carrier air forces.

ACCHAN is responsible for the English Channel and southern North Sea. Its commander, Cinchan, has his HQ at Northwood, and his commands are mainly naval but include Allied Maritime Air Force Channel Command.

AFNE (Northern Europe) is geographically divided into zones but includes no separate air command. AFCE (Central Europe) does contain separate air elements, and they are the most powerful in Western Europe: the Commander

of AAFCE (Allied Air Forces Central Europe) has his HQ at Ramstein, Germany, and he commands 2ATAF and 4ATAF. The 2nd Allied Tactical Air Force comprises the tactical airpower of Belgium and the Netherlands, plus RAF Germany and part of the Luftwaffe, and its HQ is at München-Gladbach. The 4th ATAF comprises the remainder of the airpower of the Luftwaffe, plus the USAF and CAF (Canadian Armed Forces) airpower on the continent of Western Europe, and its HQ is at Ramstein. AFSE (Southern Europe) does have a separate AAFSE (Allied Air Forces Southern Europe) command, and from Naples this controls the airpower of Italy (5ATAF), Greece (28ATAF) and Turkey, with Spain being integrated.

Many other elements of European NATO airpower are nationally controlled, or assigned to a local maritime commander, or not assigned to NATO command at all. Conversely, a few others wear two hats and can be called upon by more than one NATO commander.

This book is concerned chiefly with hardware, and it is for reasons of tasking and command structure that it excludes such aircraft as the Lockheed P-3 Orion and S-3 Viking, even though these have plenty of "attack" capability.

Sweden, Austria and Switzerland are not part of NATO, and have no

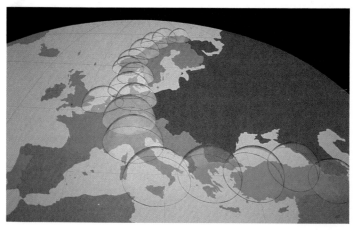

Above: The only tangible military defence system linking the NATO countries of Europe is Nadge, symbolized by 'radar hemispheres'. (Artwork was prepared before Spain, shown in blue, joined NATO.)

Above: Despite the near-abandonment of the US version, Roland remains a NATO SAM.

place in this book. France's air-power is included, though it is not assigned to NATO. The B-52, Vulcan, B-1B and FB-111A are included because all might be important in a NATO context within this book's current life. So might the AV-8B, and certainly the RAF Harrier GR-5, even though the latter is years away from service. The ACA (Agile Combat Aircraft), however, is too nebulous to merit a place. Helicopters are dealt with in a companion volume, *An Illustrated Guide to Military Helicopters*.

Vulnerability of NATO bases

Before analysing in detail NATO's air forces and the aircraft they fly, it is important to look at some of the problems concerning a subject just as fundamental as the actual hardware—where they are based.

It is without doubt that its bases are the Achilles heel of any modern air force. In World War II the Luftwaffe operated from front-line strips which, in a fluid battle situation, changed from day to day. Today the Warsaw Pact air forces

and the Swedish Flygvapen can in emergency vanish into countless preplanned locations using country roads and even unpaved surfaces as runways. Even tiny Switzerland can in emergency disperse its small air force to a dozen strips with support facilities, including hangars, cut into the sides of mountains.

NATO's formidable airpower seems, to the casual observer, to be a colossal waste of money because it can be caught, at any hour of any day, on a pitifully small number of well-known airfields.

Certainly the NATO nations have made strenuous efforts to ameliorate the effects of conventional air attack on these bases. Almost (but not quite) all have at least a machine gun pointing skywards. Many have specialist flak troops with rapid-fire cannon (in a few cases radar-directed), and a few airfields are protected by locally emplaced SAMs.

RAF Germany has a unit of the RAF Regiment at every operational airfield with eight towed Rapier fire units, which have been given blind-fire night/all-weather facilities. Rapiers of the RAF Regiment will defend USAF bases in the UK, and are expected to be ordered for bases of the 17th AF in Germany. ▶

► The French Armée de l'Air uses the Crotale SAM system in large numbers. Luftwaffe bases were to have had Roland fire units; these were cancelled and a scheme to use AIM-9L Sidewinder in a Chaparral-type installation is being studied, and the Luftwaffe's 216 Improved Hawk launchers are in some cases sited at airfields. A few NATO bases are protected to some degree by infantry-fired weapons, notably Redeye and Stinger.

In addition there has been a major sustained effort to reduce the effect of attacking aircraft which do get through. By late 1982 almost every tactical aircraft in the front-line inventory of 2 and 4ATAF, and many RAF and USAF aircraft in the UK, were matched by a Hardened Aircraft Shelter. These are concrete-floored one-plane huts constructed of reinforced concrete to any of (usually) three standard designs, with heavy end doors, intended to offer protection to the interior against direct hits with bomblets and weapons up to about 220lb (100kg) size, and against near misses with pavement-cratering or larger bombs.

In time of crisis as many aircraft as possible would spend as much time as possible inside shelters, or airborne. Further effort and cost have been devoted to the quick repair of runways and other pavements cratered by air attack. All personnel have NBC clothing.

Such measures are no more than prudent commonsense. But nothing appears to have been done to address the problem which, to the author, renders the whole of NATO's airpower (except perhaps the Harrier) a most fragile asset.

It is common knowledge that to the Warsaw Pact nuclear (and indeed other unconventional) arms are no big deal; they are just a particular range of options to be used as and when ordered. All WP troops undergo simulated nuclear and chemical warfare training surpassing anything attempted in the West. Yet it would be NATO, and not the WP, who would be on the receiving end.

At a quick count the Soviet tactical forces alone could fire 4,700 nuclear warheads with accuracy far better than the size of an airfield in the first few minutes of any conflict against Western Europe, and without touching any

Below: Patriot promises to be the greatest-ever SAM; but at what a cost in time and money!

Above: A French Jaguar outside a hardened shelter. Runways are vulnerable, though.

of the strategic weapons of the RVSN (Raketnye Voiska Strategi cheskogo Naznacheniya—Strategic Rocket Forces). NATO has no known defence against such an attack, and as 98 per cent of NATO's European combat airpower is to be found on a total of 69 bases there would be around 4,631 missiles left for a second strike.

Perhaps the simple answer is that, as NATO has announced no answer to this obvious threat, it prefers to ignore it. Such an ostrich posture appears difficult to justify when one considers the financial burden imposed on Europe's taxpayers by the aircraft featured in this book. It may be that it is tacitly assumed in NATO circles that the WP forces would only use nuclear weapons as a last resort; and so we find such assessments as those made from time to time by Western analysts who recently calculated that 89 per cent of NATO's European airpower would still be operating on the third day of World War III! In the author's view less than 5 per cent would be operating after the pre-emptive strike which would *precede* such a war.

It might not be a bad thing if NATO could take an hour or two off from its cosy assessments of how its sophisticated modern aircraft stack up against the supposed crude and outdated aircraft of the Warsaw Pact (it appears to be instinctive to undervalue Soviet hardware until we find out more about it), and instead address itself to the problem of how to make those expensive aircraft survive longer than five minutes in any European war situation.

For a start we could add a zero, and possibly two zeros, to the total of 69 major operating locations. To prepare 6,900 adequate airstrips, without causing aggravation to Western Europe's farmers or environmentalist groups, is not as ludicrously impossible as it sounds. Even in the tight little isle of Britain there are over 1,400 former air fields, many of which still have the basis of a paved runway. The rest of Europe provides quite a lot of real estate, heavily sprinkled with former airbases.

Dispersal is more cost-effective than hardening, and is good against nuclear attack as well. We are not talking about properly equipped bases, merely locations to which aircraft could be temporarily dispersed, and where convincing dummies able to fool multispectral surveillance could be located.

Yet for years NATO has done just the opposite and concentrated more and more airpower on fewer and fewer bases. Italy's AMI, for example, has completely abandoned the idea of "one gruppo, one base" ▶

15

Belgium	West Germany
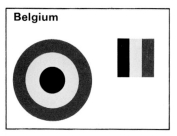	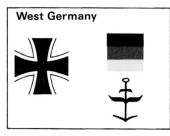

Canada	Greece
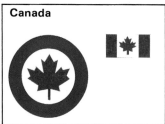	

Denmark	Italy
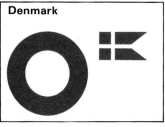	

France	Netherlands
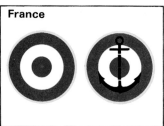	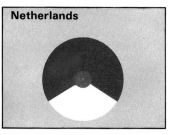

▶ and cut the number of operational airfields since 1975 from 95 to 20, of which only 11 are effective. Belgium has four and the Netherlands three. Can this really be considered viable airpower?

The present situation seems to be based on the groundless belief that the Soviet Union would not use its tactical nuclear missiles against NATO airfields. These are surely the very first and most obvious facilities against which these missiles must already be targeted.

Even the RAF's Harriers can be caught at just two airfields! Has the RAF done its homework and readied 100 remote sites where Harriers could quickly be dispersed, and where the takeoff run ends in a natural ski-jump? Apart from HMS *Invincible* (which was almost sold) and *Illustrious,* the only elements of NATO airpower in the European theatre which appear to have a chance of actually participating in the defence of Western Europe are those aboard the one (or two) carriers of the US Sixth Fleet, which do not stay in the same place.

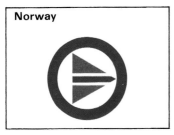

Norway

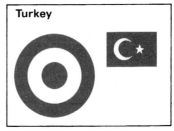

Turkey

Portugal

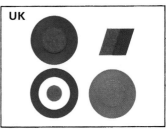

UK

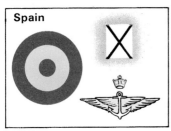

Spain

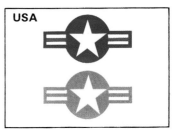

USA

Some of the insignia carried by NATO military aircraft has not changed in 60 years, but two of the technical leaders, the UK and USA, have lately conducted prolonged studies into whether such markings have much value. The so-called B-type roundel and fin flash, which eliminates white, was first used on RAF night bombers almost 60 years ago, and not only has it been restored but in the Falklands campaign the colours were toned down further (lower right UK roundel). For the same reason the regular US marking is being replaced on combat aircraft by a monochrome insignia in black or, more often, medium grey to reduce contrast.

Air forces of the NATO nations

The following is an alphabetical listing of NATO air forces as they impinge upon NATO. Iceland has no armed forces and at most NATO committee meetings votes with the majority by leaving its chair vacant. Luxembourg plays a much more active part in the Alliance, but again has no airpower (though, for purely legal reasons, the NATO fleet of 18 Boeing E-3A Sentry AWACS aircraft are registered as the property of the Grand Duchy).

Belgium

Virtually the whole of the nation's airpower is vested in the FAB (Force Aérienne Belge), or, in Flemish, the Belgisch Luchtmacht, which is part of 2ATAF. It has six main operating bases: Beauvechain (F-16, with F-104Gs still being replaced), Florennes (Mirage 5BA), Bierset (Mirage 5BA), Kleine Brogel (F-16, with F-104Gs being replaced), Brussels-Melsbroek (transports) and Brustem (trainers, including Alpha Jets). The ALFT (army light aviation) has helicopters plus seven fixed-wing Defenders. ▶

▶ The FNB (navy) has Alouettes.

Canada

Since 1975 there has been a single unified CAF (Canadian Armed Forces), or Forces Armées Canadiennes. Within the Dominion the CAF includes a large cross-the-board spectrum of airpower organized into an Air Defense Group, a Tactical Air Group, a Maritime Air Group, an Air Transport Group and an Air Reserve Group. From NATO's viewpoint the most important of these forces are the 18 CP-140 Aurora shore-based patrol/ASW aircraft and the 35 ship-based CH-124 Sea Kings. In Europe, however, Canada has since World War II maintained an important tactical presence, currently termed No 1 CAG (Canadian Air Group).

The combat element comprises 77 CF-104s tasked with offensive air-support missions as part of 4th ATAF, normally based at Baden-Söllingen, Germany. Some of these aircraft, and 20 CF-104D two-seaters, serve with 417 Sqn, the OCU at Cold Lake, Alberta. At Lahr, Germany, are two CC-132 Dash-7s assigned to 412 Sqn (the rest of 412 is at Uplands, Ottawa) and the 11 CH-136 Kiowa helicopters of 444 Sqn.

Denmark

Typical of NATO's language difficulties is the fact that RDAF (Royal Danish Air Force) is an accepted NATO title, whereas this force is actually the KDF (Kongelige Danske Flyvevaben), or Flyvevabnet (Flyvevaabnet) for short. Its tactical force is a single Flyvertaktisk Kommando, or in NATO language Tacden.

It comprises one squadron (Esk 723) of F-16s and one (Esk 726) of F-10s at Aalborg, two of F-35 Drakens (725, 729) at Karup and two of F-16s (727, 730) at Skrydstrup. Each of these Eskadriller has a nominal complement of 20 aircraft, rather than a more usual 16, because they contain two-seaters to meet the training requirement following the disbandment of training command in 1970. Other forces include C-130 and S-61 transport/SAR aircraft at Vaerlose and good

coverage with Nike Hercules and Hawk SAMs. Primary training is done on T-17 Supporters, a type also used by the small Haerens Flyvetjeneste (army flying service) along with Hughes 500M helicopters. The navy flies Lynx and Alouette helicopters.

France

Strongly nationalistic, and thus a frequent stumbling-block in international programmes (unless she can appear to be the leader of the project), France has from the outset been a full member of NATO. In 1966, however, she withdrew from the military command structure, and her forces are thus under purely national control.

Unlike all other W. European powers, the French army, navy and air force all deploy substantial nuclear firepower, the air force (l'Armée de l'Air) being responsible not only for the recallable Forces Aériennes Stratégiques (FAS) with manned bombers, but also for the 1e Groupement de Missiles Stratégiques (GMS) with two squadrons each having nine silos loaded with S3 missiles of up to 3,300km (2,050 miles) range. The FAS received 62 Mirage IVA supersonic bombers but now deploys an effective force of 32 divided into two escadres (wings) with strong tanker support and maximum dispersal.

Cafda (Commandement Air des Forces de Défense Aérienne) still has an EC (escadre de chasse, fighter wing) at Creil, north of Paris, flying the 20-year-old Mirage IIIC; the other three ECs fly the Mirage F1 and may later equip with the Mirage 2000.

Catac (Commandement Aérien Tactique) is much larger and comprises four ECs of Mirage IIIs and 5s, four of Jaguars, an ER with Mirage recon aircraft and a training EC with Alpha Jets. One EC, No 2 at Dijon, is to re-equip with the Mirage 2000 from 1984. The rest of l'Armée de l'Air comprises large transport and training forces, and an AWACS-type platform is being sought.

The Aéronautique Navale will soldier on well into the '90s with its

Above: Marineflieger Tornado with MW-1 bomblet dispenser.

two ex-RN wartime carriers in which are embarked Super Etendard attack aircraft; the ASW Alizé, Atlantic/ANG and Falcon Gardian patrol aircraft are outside the scope of this book, as are the large helicopter and light-fixed-wing forces of Alat (Aviation Légère de l'Armée de Terre, light aviation of the army.

Germany (FDR)

Largest and best-equipped of the European NATO nations, West Germany has a powerful Luftwaffe assigned partly to 2ATAF and partly to 4ATAF; the army and navy also deploy substantial air forces subordinate to national ground and naval commands (which are themselves assigned to NATO).

A new air-combat fighter has long been sought to back up the F-4F which equips two JG (fighter wings) and two JaboG (fighter/bomber wings). Four JaboG of F-104s are progressively being replaced by Tornadoes, and the two AG (recon wings) of RF-4Es are acquiring offensive power by equipping these aircraft to fly precision attack missions. Three JaboG (41, 43 and 49) have equipped with the Alpha Jet in the light-attack role, together with a training unit at Beja, Portugal. Dual Tornadoes equip the TTTE in England and a WS (Waffenschule, weapon school) at Erding in Germany. Hansa Jets are used for ECM training and VIP liaison, and numerous T-37s, T-38s,

F-4s and F-104s fly in the USA as trainers. A few of the once vast fleet of F-104s are flying in the attack, training, recon and ECM roles.

Slightly different Tornadoes are the chief combat type of the Navy's Marineflieger, progressively equipping two MFG (navy air wings); other MFGs fly the Atlantic (some in the EW role), Sea King and Lynx.The Army Heeresflieger operates hundreds of helicopters, chief types being the anti-tank BO 105P, UH-1, CH-53 and Alouette.

Greece

The Elliniki Aeroporia has, with the Turkish AF, always been one of NATO's problem areas; indeed the nation was not even an active NATO member in 1974-80.The El's combat strength, part of AFSE, is the 28th Tactical Air Force, made up of seven pterighe (wings). Each of these has a liaison flight of T-33s and AB 205s, but the combat strength comprises the following: 110a Pterix, Larissa, one mire (sqn) each of A-7H, F-4E and mixed RF-4E/RF-84F; 111a, Nea Ankhialos, two mire F-5A/B; 113a, Thessalonika-Mikra, one mire F-5/RF-5; 114a, Tanagra, two mire Mirage F1-CG with Magic AAMs; 115a, Soudha Bay, two mire A-7H with AIM-9L self-defence AAMs; 116a, Araxos, two mire F/TF-104G; ▶

19

▶ and 117a, Andravida, two mire F-4E. The EI has many secondary types, including C-130s and T-2E jet trainers. The army and navy fly mainly helicopters.

Italy
The AMI (Aeronautica Militare Italiano) provides the bulk of 5ATAF, and has a substantial force of effective and aggressively flown aircraft despite sustained—indeed worsening—problems caused by a critical shortage of money, a poor national economy and a frequently changed government teetering on the brink of a Communist majority.

Its main combat strength is organized into 12 stormi (regiments) each comprising one or two gruppi (squadrons) ostensibly of 16 to 25 aircraft but effectively shrunk to 12 to 18. Thus the order of battle reads (in numerical stormo order): 2 Stormo, Treviso, two gruppi G91R; 3S, Verona, two gruppi F/RF-104; 4S, Grosseto, one gruppo F-104S; 5S, Rimini, two gruppi F-104S; 6S, Ghedi, one gruppo (No 154) Tornado; 8S, Cervia, one gruppo G91Y; 9S, Grazzianise, one gruppo F-104S; 14S, Pratica di Mare, two gruppi MB 326, MB 339, PD 808 and G222, all ECM platforms; 32S, Brindisi, one gruppo G91Y; 36S, Giola del Colle, two gruppi F-104S in strike role, one (156) being part-converted to Tornado; 51S, Istrana (Treviso), two gruppi F-104S, one about to convert to Tornado; and 53S, Cameria, one gruppo F-104S interceptors.

Two gruppi fly Atlantics in the ASW role under the control of the Marinavia, which flies helicopters. The ALE (army light aviation) has large forces of helicopters, and a few fixed-wing lightplanes.

Netherlands
The KLu (Koninklijke Luchtmacht) has a number of built-in headwinds, such as an officially recognised trade union for its other ranks, but manages to deploy effective airpower as part of 2ATAF, using three types of fighter and four airfields.

At Leeuwarden are squadrons Nrs 322 and 323 equipped with the F-16; at Volkel are Nr 312, with the last F-104Gs, and Nrs 306 (tac-recon) and 311 with F-16s; at Gilze Rijen are Nrs 314 and 316 with NF-5As; and at Twenthe is 315 with NF-5As and also Nr 313, the pilot OCU with the NF-5B. In the later part of the decade the KLu combat strength will rest on one type, the F-16. Pilot training to wings standard is done in Canada and the USA.

The Marine Luchtvaartdienst operates Orions, Atlantics and Lynx.

Norway
The KNL (Kongelige Norske Luftforsvaret), styled RNorAF in NATO English-language publications, is another NATO force which will

Below: Few would dispute that the F-16 (KLu aircraft shown) is ideal for Western Europe.

probably soon rely entirely on the F-16 for its tactical firepower. 331 Sqn flies the F-16A/B from Bodo; 332 flies the same mix from Rygge; 334 is converting from Bullpup-armed F-104Gs in the anti-ship role to the F-16 which will eventually carry the locally produced Penguin 3 missile; 336 still operates F-5As, as well as the camera-equipped RF-5As passed on by disbanded 717 Sqn; and 338 flies F-5As from Orland. The missing numbers are 333 (P-3B Orions) and 337 (Lynx), while 718 is a training squadron with F-5Bs.

Portugal

The FAP (Forca Aérea Portuguesa) has been quite literally the poorest in Western Europe, and it makes no contribution to NATO whatsoever. It once had a "squadron" of four SP-2H Neptunes (ex-Netherlands KLu) which operated as part of ACLANT, and has been trying to replace these with P-3 Orions ex-USN.

The only modern fighting aircraft are 20 A-7P Corsair II attack machines, which are refurbished ex-USN A-7As fitted with A-7E avionics; they equip Escuadra (squadron) 302 at BA-5 Monte Real, replacing F-86 Sabres. Another 30, including six two-seaters, may be on the way by the time this book appears. The only other significant force is at BA-6 Montijo, where Grupo 52, Esc 301, uses ex-Luftwaffe G91Rs armed with Sidewinders to hold the fort in the intercept role until a fighter can be obtained.

Other equipment includes C-130s, CASA Aviocars and helicopters, and in 1982 it was unofficially stated that the FAP was negotiating for five Brazilian EMB-111 coastal surveillance aircraft.

Spain

Details have not yet emerged of how, if at all, Spain's airpower will be assigned to NATO command, but it is considerable. The EdA (Ejercito del Aire, army of the air) organizes its combat strength into four commands (manda).

El Mando Aéreo de Combate has fighters for home defence, controlled by the Combat Grande (Nadge type) defence system and comprising Esc (Escuadron) 111 at Manises (Mirage III, to be replaced from 1986 by F-18s); Esc 121 at Torrejon (F-4CR and RF-4C); and Esc 141 at Los Llanos (Mirage F1.CE).

El Mando Aéreo Tactico has Esc 211 (SF-/SRF-5A/B) and Esc 214 (HA 220 Super Saeta) both at Morón in the attack role and Esc 221 with Orions.

El Mando Aéreo de Canarias (Canary Islands) has a base at Gando housing Esc 462 (Mirage F1.CE) and Esc 464 (SF-/SRF-5A/B) as well as squadrons flying Aviocars, Super Pumas and other types.

El Mando Aéreo de Transporte flies C-130s, KC-130 tankers and other types.

The Arma Aérea de la Armada (naval air force) has Esc 008 equipped with AV-8A/TAV-8A Harriers, due for replacement from 1987 by AV-8B Harrier IIs. Other types include AH-1G Cobras, Sea Kings and ASW Agusta Bells.

Turkey

Despite its terrible economy, this enormous country is so vital, so threatened and possessed of such military manpower that, with help from other NATO members, it has built up a tactical air force of considerable strength. In bygone years it was a dumping ground for what everyone else cast off. The process continues, and the hangars are jammed with surplus F-100s; indeed even the F-104Gs have been arriving in such numbers that not all of them have yet been put into service with a pilot to fly them, but most of these have actually been paid for (albeit at little more than scrap value), and Turkey bought its F-104S force new from Aeritalia.

As this book is written, in early 1983, Turkey's wish to buy, or better still build, F-16s has not been settled. Tusas, the proposed Turkish aircraft industry, has been argued over for 13 years, and has at last made a modest start with the industrial partner most willing to ▶

► help, Northrop (other companies agreed with the American who said "The world needs another planemaker like it needs a hole in the head"). The first licence-assembled F-5E finally rolled out in 1982, two years late, and Tiger IIs should replace F-5A/B aircraft by 1987.

The THK (Turk Hava Kuvvetleri) deploys its fighting strength in two TAFs. The 1st Tac Air Force comprises: 111 Filo (sqn), F-100C/D/F; 112, F/RF-5A; and 113, F/RF-4E, all at Eskisehir; 131, 132, both with F-100 (being replaced by F-104) at Konya; 141, F-104G, and 142, F-104S interceptors, both at Murted; 161, F-5A/B, and 162, F-4E, both at Bandirma; and 191, F-10-4G, and 192, F-5A/B, both at Balikesir. The 2nd TAF (no relation to 2ATAF) has 151, 152, F-5A/B, at Merzifon; 171, 172, F-4E, both at Erhac-Malataya; and 181, F-5A/B, 182, F-104S, and 183, RF-5A, all at Diyarbakir.

Air Support Command has both Transalls and C-130s, the navy still uses S-2 Trackers as well as helicopters, and the army has both helicopters and fixed-wing but has so far not managed to build anti-tank Tow-Defenders.

United Kingdom

The sudden Falklands conflict both arrested the previous pattern of "defence cuts" and reminded the MoD that it must never be 100 per cent polarized around NATO. This should do the RAF and Fleet Air Arm a power of good.

The RAF's airpower is divided into RAF Germany and Strike Command. The former, a major element of 2ATAF with HQ at Rheindahlen, comprises two squadrons (3 and 4) of Harriers; 2, 17, 20 and 31 of Jaguars; 15 and 16 of Buccaneers; and 19 and 92 of Phantoms.

Strike Command comprises four groups. No 1 (Bomber) Group has lost virtually all of its Vulcans, apart from six K.2 tankers, the six squadrons progressively re-equipping with the Tornado GR.1. Nos 12 and 216 Sqns fly Buccaneers in maritime attack, and 208 in land attack, and with updating the former two units may go on throughout the decade. Two squadrons (55, 57) fly Victor K.2 tankers. Canberras, Nimrod R.1s and electronic warfare expertise is concentrated at Wyton, where there is a small photo-recon unit (replacing No 39 Sqn) with Canberra PR.9s. No 11 (Fighter) Group has 23, 29, 56 and 111 flying Phantoms, with 64 serving as the OCU, and No 43 on the ex-RN Phantom FG.1; 5 and 11 will fly Lightnings until 1985, and in 1983 No 8 was to trade its aged Shackletons for Nimrod AEW.3s.

In 1984 No 11 Group will be merged into No 1. No 18 (Maritime) Group flies Nimrods and helicopters. No 38 Group is the UK's Rapid Deployment Force, comprising 1 Sqn, Harriers; 6, 41 and 54, Jaguars; and 63, 79 and 234 with Hawks (and a few Hunters), about 90 of the Hawks being tasked not only with attack training but also, with AIM-9L Sidewinders, with defending UK airspace. Among 38 Group's varied transport force is the squadron of VC 10 K.2 and K.3 tankers.

The Fleet Air Arm's Sea Harrier squadrons (800, 801 and 899) all fought over the Falklands; one more will be formed when 14 additional aircraft are delivered. The remainder of the FAA, and most of the AAC (Army Air Corps) and Marine Commando Air Squadrons, are rotary-wing.

USA

American airpower is deployed among the USAF (across the board, and including all global or inter-theatre force), the USN (shore-based and seagoing, the latter organized into 13 extremely powerful Carrier Air Groups), the USMC (limited to close-support and supply of amphibious forces) and USA (rotary-wing on a gigantic scale, with very small fixed-wing strength notably including about 200 OV-1 Mohawks).

President Reagan has restored an improved B-1 as a weapon for the inventory, restored the C-5 as a production aircraft (with extra KC-10s) instead of the new C-17, and created a Rapid Deployment Force for swift transport to trouble spots. There is no room in this book for a detailed breakdown of even the combat units of the USAF (the reader is referred to the companion volume, *An Illustrated Guide to the Modern USAF*).

The most important US airpower to European NATO nations is USAFE (US Air Force Europe), which is a separate Air Force command organized into the 3rd, 16th and 17th Air Forces and with HQ at Ramstein AB, Germany, and bases in Germany, Greece, Italy, the Netherlands, Spain, Turkey and the UK.

The 3rd AF has HQ at Mildenhall, England, and includes the 10th TRW (RF-4C and TR-1, with 17th TRW as support unit) and 527th TFT "Aggressor" Sqn (F-5E) at Alconbury, the 20th TFW (F-111E) at Upper Heyford, the 48th TFW (F-111F) at Lakenheath, the 81st TFW (A-10A) at Bentwaters/Wood- ▶

Below: Without this aircraft the recovery of the Falklands would have been impossible.

bridge, with detachments at six forward bases in Germany, and the 513th TAW (C-130, EC-135 etc) at Mildenhall; support units at Mildenhall manage KC-135s rotated to Mildenhall/Fairford and various other types including occasional SR-71s. At Woodbridge the 67ARRS (HC-130, HH-53) provides SAR for the whole of USAFE.

The 16th AF has HQ at Torrejón AB, Spain, and includes the 401st TFW (F-4C) at Torrejón and 406th TFT wing (a holding unit) with F-4s, A-10s and F-15s at Zaragoza, with support for visiting KC-135s.

The 17th AF has HQ at Sembach AB, Germany, and includes the 26th TRW (RF-4C) at Zweibrücken, the 32nd TFS (F-15) at Camp Amsterdam, Soesterberg, the 36th TFW (F-15) at Bitburg, the 50th TFW (F-16) at Hahn, the 52nd TFW (F-4D/F-4G) at Spangdahlem, the 86th TFW (F-4E, T-39) at Ramstein, the 435th TAW (C-9, MC-130E) at Rhein-Main, the 601st TCW (O-2, OV-10, TR-1, CH-53) at Sembach and various support units.

The US Navy airpower is based chiefly in the continental USA, or afloat in the Pacific or Atlantic Fleets, but the C-in-C US Navy Europe (HQ, London) has major subordinate forces including the Sixth Fleet (Gaeta, Italy) and Fleet Air Mediterranean (Naples), while aircraft from other commands often visit Europe. Fleet Air Med manages patrol squadrons (mainly P-3C, EP-3E) on TDY at Rota, Spain, and Sigonella, Sicily, while transport squadron VP-24 supports the Sixth

Fleet with C-130Fs, CT-39Gs and COD C-2A Greyhounds.

The US Army has substantial helicopter forces in Germany but none of its fixed-wing types appear in this book. Readers are referred to Salamander's *The US War Machine*.

NATO's future aircraft

Included in this book are all the manned fixed-wing fighter and attack aircraft of which details are known and which are planned to enter NATO service during the 1980s. Modern combat aircraft take a long time to design and develop. One has only to recall the apparent surprise of Western defence analysts at the "primitive" nature of the MiG-25 Foxbat which was examined at Hakodate Airport in September 1976 to see that this basic fact is often forgotten. The analysts should have remembered that the MiG-25 was flying prior to 1965 and therefore must have been designed prior to 1960, so of course its fundamental technology was that of the 1960s and not that of 1976.

Not only amateur enthusiasts but also the professionals in military airpower often overlook the vital time factor. What we do today cannot have much effect until the 1990s. The airpower NATO deploys today is because of decisions taken not in the 1970s but the 1960s.

There is an almost childish

Below: Little credence need be given to futuristic strike fighters—even from Boeing!

amount of fashion in the design of combat aircraft—or perhaps it would be fairer to the designers to say there is fashion in the specifications written by the air staffs. In the 1950s aircraft first had to exceed Mach 1, then Mach 2, and by 1957 the richer nations went for Mach 3.

Odd man out was Britain, which in 1957 unilaterally announced that manned combat aircraft were obsolete and that the RAF was "unlikely to require" any to follow the Lightning, which with extreme reluctance was permitted to continue "because it has gone too far to cancel".

After 1960 everything had to be V/STOL—and very sensibly too, because airfield-based airpower is simply meaningless—but, partly because V/STOL tended to mean using British engines, this was effectively withered by the USA, and in particular by the USAF, though the Marines managed to keep one small branch still alive.

The mind boggles at the thought of American taxpayers forking out 30 billion dollars for F-15 Eagles alone, every single one of which (except for the few which happen to be in the air) can be wiped out at

Above: BAe Warton's mock-up of an Agile Combat Aircraft at least has some funds behind it.

the touch of a few Russian buttons.

Giving aircraft swing-wings helps greatly, because this cuts down the field length by about half. This was fashionable in the West in the 1960s, but today is regarded sensibly only by the bad guys who fly their tactical aircraft from places other than airfields. By the 1970 era fashion had switched to the acronym RPV, because it is easy to demonstrate that a remotely-piloted vehicle can outfly any equivalent aircraft burdened by a heavy man in a heavy ejection seat in a heavily protected cockpit.

Today we are almost back to square one, with combat aircraft that don't have to have supersonic performance, or V/STOL, or swing wings or remote pilots.

Is it not remarkable that the USAF, the world leader in combat-aircraft technology, can not only forget about V/STOL but also equip squadrons in Europe with a new and extremely costly tactical reconnaissance aircraft which flies no faster than a Spitfire, while its future long-distance bomber, de- ▶

signed to penetrate a thousand miles into hostile territory, should retain supersonic performance and swing wings only because it would cost even more to eliminate these features?

The new buzz-word is "stealth", to describe a wide range of shapes, coatings and technologies to try to make aircraft invisible to the enemy. The invisible aircraft was fashionable in the early 1930s, and the Russians even tried to build one. Today by "invisible" is meant having a minimal radar signature; how far stealth technology is also concerned with the suppression of IR emissions has received less public discussion, but clearly the ideal future combat aircraft has to try to be as invisible as possible over as much of the electromagnetic spectrum as possible. We are thus concerned with longer wavelengths such as radar (which today gets down to the millimetric waveband), and with the much shorter wavelengths of IR (heat) and visible light.

There is no doubt whatsoever that stealth technology, at present applied only to a single extremely sophisticated strategic bomber being developed chiefly by Northrop for USAF service after 1990, will gradually become the central feature of all military aircraft.

Present preoccupation with turn radius, SEP (specific excess power, a measure of spare propulsive energy) and agility will cease to be very important because future missiles—fired from other aircraft or from land or ship launchers—will clobber all aircraft, irrespective of how good or bad they are in these matters.

In the past, traditional dogfight manoeuvrability has been important in preventing the bad guy from ever getting within "parameters" (a position from which he can successfully launch a missile or engage with a gun). Thanks to digital microelectronics about the size of a pack of playing cards, future AAMs will find their target provided it is within range, even if they are launched in the wrong direction entirely. The RAF's belief in a self-defence AAM fired to the rear is based on a naïve belief that the fighter of the 1990s will have to get on its opponent's tail.

At present we are witnessing the last chapter in the long history of manoeuvrable fighters. The USAF professes still to be polarized around agility, as witnessed by the Grumman X-29A with its swept-

Below: US DoD sketch of an FSW (Forward-swept wing) combat aircraft for 1992.

forward wing, the F-16AFTI which can dart up, down or sideways without changing direction, and the Rockwell HiMAT (highly manoeuvrable aircraft technology) which goes for agility at the expense of everything else. Before too long the penny (or rather cent) will drop, and even the USAF will realize that agility gets you nowhere. The things that count are small physical size, RAM (radar-absorbent materials), and the best command of the electromagnetic spectrum.

So, to recap: NATO airpower of the 1990s will have to be as elusive as possible. It certainly cannot be tied to the handful of known airfields, or we may as well save

Above: Another American idea of how a 1990s fighter might be.

our money. It must be widely dispersed in literally thousands of locations, 95 per cent of which at any given moment have nothing there. It must be as nearly as possible invisible to hostile reconnaissance platforms looking down from above. It must also be as invisible as possible, at all EM wavelengths, when it is in flight.

This is a challenge that the 16 nations could work on together; it is too big for any one of them.

Below: In contrast the Grumman X-29A actually exists, though this was drawn before it flew.

Aeritalia/Aermacchi/ EMBRAER AMX

AMX

Origin: Joint programme by Aeritalia (Combat Aircraft Group), Naples, Italy, Aermacchi SpA, Varese, Italy, and EMBRAER, São José dos Campos, Brazil.

Type: Single-seat attack.

Engine: One 11,030lb (5003kg) thrust Rolls-Royce Spey 807 turbofan produced under licence by Alfa Romeo and Piaggio.

Dimensions: Span (excl AAMs and rails) 29ft 1½in (8.88m); length 44ft 6¼in (13.57m); wing area 226.0sq ft (21.0m²).

Weights: Empty 14,330lb (6,500kg); maximum 26,455lb (12,000kg).

Performance: (estimated) to fly lo-lo-lo mission with tanks plus 3,000lb (1,360kg) ordnance at Mach 0.75-plus, with dash at Mach 0.95 (722mph, 1,162km/h) with radius of 208 miles (335km); field length 3,000ft (914m).

Armament: Internal gun (Italy, one 20mm M61A-1 with transverse ammo drum; Brazil, two 30mm DEFA 554); twin fuselage pylons each rated at 1,000lb (454kg); inboard wing pylons each rated at 2,000lb (907kg) plumbed for 220gal (1,000lit) tanks; outboard wing pylons each rated at 1,000lb (454kg) plumbed for 100gal (455lit) tanks; wingtip rails for AIM-9L or similar AAMs, max ordnance not stated but for very short range theoretically 8,000lb (3,629kg) plus AAMs.

History: Project started 1977; first flight due 1983, delivery from 1986.

Users: Expected initially to be Italy and Brazil, plus export customers.

Deployment: Throughout the early 1970s Aeritalia (previously Fiat Aviazione) studied projects which could replace the company's G91 light attack and reconnaissance aircraft. The choice fell on a new-generation aircraft in the same class. This still leaves Italy looking for a new interceptor and air-combat fighter, but the AMX (the designation stemmed from Aeritalia-Aermacchi experimental, the second Italian partner joining the project in mid-1978) was planned in collaboration with the AMI (Italian air force), which has announced a requirement for 187 for the re-equipment of eight gruppi (squadrons). AMX promises to be an extremely cost-effective multi-role aircraft in the class of the Skyhawk. Though the first had not flown as this book went to press, it is clear it will have internal passive warning receivers (British-style, on the fin) and will be large enough to carry substantial and varied offensive loads, ECM pods and tanks, with full-span slats and carbon-fibre double-slotted flaps for short field length. No radar is specified, except a ranging sight, but an inertial nav/attack system and commendably advanced communications and other avionics will be installed, and a Martin-Baker Mk 10 seat. Two-seat and multisensor recon versions are planned. AMI operations are scheduled to begin in spring 1987, and sales to other members of the Alliance look promising.

Above: The latest Aeritalia artwork illustrating AMX when this book went to press in early 1983; it is based on a model photo.

Above: The two mock-ups have had numerous foreign visitors.

Below: Profile of AMX. Eventual NATO service is probable, and development of variants is anticipated.

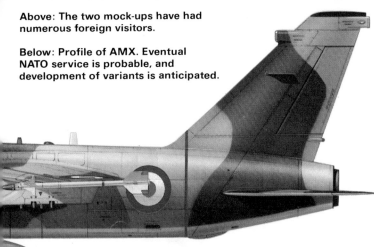

Aeritalia G91

G91R, G91T, G91PAN and G91Y

Origin: Fiat SpA (now Aeritalia SpA).

Type: G91R and Y, single-seat tactical reconnaissance/fighter; G91T two-seat weapon trainer; G91PAN, single-seat aerobatic display fighter.

Engines: (G91R, T and PAN) one 5,000lb (2,268kg) thrust Rolls-Royce Orpheus 80302 turbojet; (G91Y) two General Electric J85-13A augmented turbojets each rated at 4,080lb (1,850kg) with full afterburner.

Dimensions: Span (G.91R, T, PAN) 28ft 1in (8.57m);a (G91Y) 29ft 6½in (9.01m); length (G91R, PAN) 33ft 9¼in (10.31m); (G91T, Y) 38ft 3½in (11.67m); height (G91R, PAN) 13ft 1½in (4m); (G91T, Y) 14ft 6in (4.43m); wing area 176.74sq ft (16.42m²).

Weights: Empty (G91R) typically 7,275lb (3,300kg), (G91Y) 8,598lb (3,900kg); maximum loaded (G91R) 12,500lb (5,695kg), (G91Y) 19,180lb (8,700kg).

Performance: Maximum speed (G91R) 675mph (1,086km/h), (G91Y) 690mph (1,110km/h); initial climb (G91R) 6,000ft (1,829m) /min, (G91Y) 17,000ft (5,180m)/min; service ceiling (G91R) 43,000ft (13,106m), (G91Y) 41,000ft (12,500m); combat radius at sea level (G91R) 196 miles (315km), (G91Y) 372 miles (600km); ferry range (G91R) 1,150 miles (1,850km), (G91Y) 2,175 miles (3,500km).

Armament: (G91R/1) four 0.5in Colt-Browning machine guns, each with 300 rounds, and underwing racks for ordnance load up to 500lb (227kg); (G91R/3) two 30mm DEFA 552 cannon, each with 125 rounds, and underwing racks for ordnance up to 1,000lb (454kg); (G91Y) two DEFA 552, underwing load up to 4,000lb (1,814kg).

History: First flight 9 August 1956; (G91R) December 1958; (G91Y prototype) 27 December 1966; (production G91Y) June 1971.

Users: (G91Y) Italy; (earlier versions) Italy, Portugal.

Above: Orpheus-powered G91 variants are no longer in front-line service with 32° Stormo, but still fly with other groups.

Deployment: In December 1953 NATO announced a specification for a light tactical strike fighter. It was to be robust, simple to maintain and capable of operation from rough advanced airstrips, yet had to reach Mach 0.92 and be able to deliver conventional or tactical nuclear weapons. Despite arguments from France the winner was Italy's G91, and Italy deployed 98 G91R/1 and 102 G91T while Germany built 294 under licence and deployed an inventory force of 50 R/3, 50 R/4 and 44 T. These gave good service, and Italy's AMI still flies strike/recon missions with two gruppi (14 and 103 of the 2° Stormo at Treviso San Angelo) as well as the national aerobatic team (313 gruppo) with the PAN version. The Luftwaffe, how-ever, had by late 1982 withdrawn its last G91R, the replacement being the attack version of the Alpha Jet. Almost all the German survivors are now in Portugal, where 42R and 8T equip Esc 301 at BA-6 Montijo. Such is Portugal's shortage of fighters that these have to fulfil the interception task, with Sidewinders, as well as their basic attack mission (a task which they are incapable of fulfilling, even in daylight). Italy went on to build 65 of the more powerful and much more-capable G91Y version, and this still equips 101 Gruppo (8° Stormo) and 13 Gruppo (32° Stormo), both at Cervia San Giorgio. Roughly equivalent to a Skyhawk, they will be replaced from 1986 by the new AMX.

Left: Looking similar to earlier versions, the G91Y brought a major increase in all-round combat capability.

Left: The air force of Portugal is more critically short of money than any of the others. It has no modern fighter, and these ex-Luftwaffe G91R light attack aircraft are also tasked with the national-defence interception of all intruders!

BAe Buccaneer

Buccaneer S.2B.

Origin: Hawker Siddeley Aviation (formerly Blackburn Aircraft, now British Aerospace), UK.

Type: Two-seat attack and reconnaissance.

Engines: Two 11,030lb (5,003kg) Rolls-Royce Spey 101 turbofans.

Dimensions: Span 44ft (13.41m); length 63ft 5in (19.33m); height 16ft 3in (4.95m); wing area 514.7sq ft (47.82m^2).

Weights: Empty about 30,000lb (13,610kg); maximum loaded 62,000lb (28,123kg).

Performance: Maximum speed 690mph (1,110km/h) at sea level; range on typical hi-lo-hi strike mission with weapon load 2,300 miles (3,700km).

Armament: Rotating bomb door carries four 1,000lb (454kg) bombs or multi-sensor reconnaissance pack or 440gal tank; four wing pylons each stressed to 3,000lb (1,361kg), compatible with very wide range of guided and/or free-fall missiles. Total internal and external stores load 16,000lb (7,257kg).

History: First flight (NA.39) 30 April 1958 (production S.1) 23 January 1962 (prototype S.2) 17 May 1963 (production S.2) 5 June 1964; final delivery late 1975.

Users: UK (RAF).

Deployment: After the notorious "Defence White Paper" of April 1957, which proclaimed manned combat aircraft obsolete, the Blackburn B.103, built to meet the naval attack specification NA.39, was the only new British military aircraft that was not cancelled. Designed for carrier operation, its ▶

Above right: Firing rockets from an RAF Buccaneer S.2, a first-class aircraft always crippled by lack of proper avionic funds.

Right: 'Bucc' loaded with Paveway smart bomb and one of the ALQ-101 ECM pods bought secondhand at a supposed bargain price.

Below: Today Buccaneers wear B-type roundels and have a few equipment updates. Note fox's head badge of No 12 Squadron.

▶ wing and tail were dramatically reduced in size as a result of powerful tip-to-tip supercirculation (BLC, boundary-layer control) achieved by blasting hot compressed air bled from the engines from narrow slits. The S.1 (strike Mk 1) was marginal on power, but the greatly improved S.2 was a reliable and formidable aircraft. The first 84 were ordered by the Royal Navy and most were transferred to RAF Strike Command, designated S.2B when converted to launch Martel missiles. The RAF signed in 1968 for 43 new S.2Bs with adequate equipment, including a refuelling probe which is never used in front-line service in Germany. Within the limits of crippling budgets the RAF Buccaneers have been updated by a few improved avionics, and have gradually been recognised as among the world's best long-range interdiction aircraft. When carrying a 4,000lb (1,814kg) bombload a 'Bucc' at full power is faster than a Mirage, Phantom or F-16 at low level, and burns less fuel per mile. Many Red Flag exercises have demonstrated that a well-flown example is among the most difficult of all today's aircraft to shoot down. On most occasions an intercepting aircraft has failed to get within missile- or gun-firing parameters before having to abandon the chase because of low fuel state. Almost universally the Buccaneer aircrews consider that "the only replacement for a Buccaneer in the 1990s will be another Buccaneer, with updated avionics".

Buccaneers equip 15 and 16 Sqns of RAF Germany (2 ATAF) at Laarbruch in the land attack role, and these are progressively being replaced by Tornado GR.1s in 1983-5 (with replacement of Jaguar squadrons as well, RAF Germany will in effect gain one extra squadron). Tornados will also (despite the wishes of their crews, so popular is the present aircraft) replace 208 Sqn, No 1 Group, at Honington. The other two UK Buccaneer units, 12 and 216, are tasked with maritime patrol and will go on well into the 1990s. All they want is better avionics, not only internal (and a new nav/attack system is due in 1984) but also better ECM than the external ALQ-101 pod. Their main anti-ship weapon will be Sea Eagle (see companion volume, *Airborne Missiles*).

Above: RAF training sorties eventually turn out superb tactical attack pilots. Here four aircraft from 208 sqn get under the radar in the UK.

Below: Another aircraft from 208 seen over British terrain of a different nature; it could fly at full power under those electricity grid cables!

BAe Harrier

Harrier GR.3 and T.4

Origin: Hawker Siddeley Aviation (now British Aerospace), UK.

Type: Single-seat STOVL tactical attack and reconnaissance; (T.4) dual trainer or special missions.

Engine: One 21,500lb (9,752kg) thrust Rolls-Royce Pegasus 103 vectored-thrust turbofan.

Dimensions: Span 25ft 3in (7.7m), (with bolt-on tips, 29ft 8in); length (GR.3) 47ft 2in (14.38m), (T.4) 57ft 3in (17.45m); height (GR.3) 11ft 3in (3.43m); (T.4) 13ft 8in (4.17m); wing area 201.1sq ft (18.68m²).

Weights: Empty (GR.3) 12,200lb (5,533kg); (T.4) 13,600lb (6,168kg); maximum (non-VTOL) 26,000lb (11,793kg).

Performance: Maximum speed over 737mph (1,186km/h, Mach 0.972) at low level; maximum dive Mach number 1.3; initial climb (VTOL weight) 50,000ft (15,240m)/min; service ceiling, over 50,000ft (15,240m); tactical radius on strike mission without drop tanks (hi-lo-hi) 260 miles (418km); ferry range 2,070 miles (3,300km).

Armament: All external, with many options. Under-fuselage strakes each replaceable by pod containing one 30mm Aden or similar gun, with 150 rounds. Five or seven stores pylons, centre and two inboard each rated at 2,000lb (907kg), outers at 650lb (295kg) and tips (if used) at 220lb (100kg) for Sidewinder AAMs, first fitted during the Falklands crisis. Normal load 5,300lb (2,400kg), but 8,000lb (3,630kg) has been flown.

History: First hover (P.1127) 21 October 1960; (development Harrier) 31 August 1966; (Harrier GR.1) 28 December 1967; (T.2) 24 April 1969; squadron service (GR.1) 1 April 1969. Note, GR.1 and T.2 updated to GR.3 and T.4.

User: UK (RAF).

Deployment: When the experimental P.1127 got daylight under its wheels in 1960 the RAF showed not the slightest interest (in any case, British combat aircraft were taboo; they had been officially pronounced obsolete). Gradually the RAF did show interest in a much more powerful Mach 2 aircraft, the P.1154, but in 1964 this was cancelled. The Government did, however, permit the development of a much smaller subsonic aircraft, and this became the Harrier, basically a machine of classic simplicity which pioneered the entire concept of STOVL (short takeoff, vertical landing) combat operations, and the sustained mounting of close-support and recon missions from dispersed sites in many parts of Europe.

Though the Harrier is small it has better range and weapon load than a Hunter, and it has also rather surprisingly emerged as an air-combat ▶

Top: A superb action photo of RAF Harrier GR.3s on a typical training sortie over Scotland; bird strike is the main problem.

Above: Harrier GR.3s of No 4 Sqn carry centreline recce pod with five cameras (also here, two tanks and two rocket pods).

Left: GR.3s of No 1 Sqn from Wittering sprayed with water-based winter camouflage for NATO Mobile Force exercises in Norway.

► adversary of extreme difficulty. Though not designed as a fighter, its combination of small size, unusual shape, lack of visible smoke and unique agility conferred by the ability to vector the engine thrust direction (to make 'impossible' square turns, violent deceleration or unexpected vertical movements without change of attitude) make even the original Harrier a most unpopular opponent for any modern interceptor. The RAF Harrier GR.3 has an inertial nav/attack system, laser ranger and marked-target seeker and fin-mounted passive warning receivers; it is planned to instal internal ECM (unlikely before 1985). RAF Germany has two squadrons (3 and 4) at Gütersloh, while in 38 Group (in 1984 to merge into 1 Group) are No 1 Sqn and 233 OCU, both at Wittering. All these units are vastly experienced, No 1 having played a central role in the recovery of the Falklands and many RAF Harrier pilots having fought with RN Sea Harrier units. The Harrier has proved a most versatile and useful aircraft, its shortcomings of limited payload/pylon space being fully rectified in the GR.5 version.

Top right: Rippling rockets at Sardinia from a GR.3 (actually the first production aircraft) from No 3 Sqn. The SNEB pods were backed up by 2in rockets over Falklands for RN compatibility.

Right: Close-up of the pre-Falklands laser nose of a GR.3 from No 1 Sqn in Norway, showing crude winter coat which was washed off after return to Wittering. GR.5 pilots will sit higher.

Below: In practice Harriers almost never do a true VTOL. This late 1982 shot shows the wake behind an arrival in wet weather.

BAe Hawk

P.1182 Hawk T.1

Origin: British Aerospace, UK.

Type: Two-seat trainer and light interceptor.

Engine: One 5,340lb (2,422kg) Rolls-Royce/Turboméca Adour 151 turbofan.

Dimensions: Span 30ft 10in (9.4m); length (over probe) 39ft 2½in (11.95m); height 13ft 5in (4.09m); wing area 179.64sq ft (16.69m²).

Weights: empty 7,450lb (3,379kg); loaded (trainer, clean) 12,000lb (5,443kg), (attack mission) 16,260lb (7,375kg).

Performance: Maximum speed 630mph (1,014km/h) at low level; Mach number in shallow dive 1.1; initial climb 6,000ft (1,830m)/min; service ceiling 50,000ft (15,240m); range on internal fuel 750 miles (1,207km); endurance with external fuel 3hr.

Armament: Three or five hard-points (two outboard being optional) each rated at 1,000lb (454kg), (export Hawk 6,800lb/3,085kg weapon load); centreline point normally equipped with 30mm gun pod and ammunition; intercept role, two AIM-9L Sidewinder.

History: First flight 21 August 1974; service delivery 1976.

Users: UK (RAF).

Deployment: The only new all-British military aircraft for 15 years, the Hawk serves as a model of the speed and success that can be achieved when an experienced team is allowed to get on with the job. The RAF ordered 175, all of which were delivered by 1982, equipping No 4 FTS at Valley in the advanced pilot training role (replacing the Gnat and Hunter) and also with No 1 TWU (Tac Weapons Unit) at Brawdy, and No 2 TWU at Chivenor, in the weapon training role. RAF Hawks normally do not have the outer pylons fitted but these could be added in hours. By late 1982 RAF Hawks had flown 170,000 hours, with the lowest accident record for any known military jet in history. It cut defect rates by 70 per cent whilst halving maintenance man-hours per flight hour. Despite the aircraft's greater size and power, fuel burn has been dramatically reduced compared with the Gnat. Hawks also equip the Red Arrows aerobatic display team, again establishing an unprecedented record for troublefree operation. In the weapon-training role aircraft are routinely turned around between sorties in 15 minutes by teams of four armourers. In 1981 it was announced that, to back up RAF Strike Command's very limited fighter defence forces, about 90 Hawks would be equipped to fire AIM-9L Sidewinders in the light interception role. Under current planning about 72 are actually armed with the missiles. In addition the Hawk was selected in 1981 as the future undergraduate pilot trainer of the US Navy, as the T-45A with full carrier gear and the T-45B for naval land training. BAe is marketing the Hawk 100 series as a dedicated multirole attack aircraft with both seats retained and fitted with nav/attack systems related to those of the F-16A.

Above: Rocket practice by a Hawk T.1 of No 1 Tactical Weapons Unit (234 Sqn), RAF Brawdy. The centreline gun pod is not fitted.

Above: Hawk T.1 trainers from RAF No 4 FTS flying over Caernarvon.

Left: Hawks of No 1 TWU are based at Brawdy and bear the insignia of 234 Sqn (seen here) and 79 Sqn. Further Hawks are based at Chivenor with 63 Sqn (2 TWU).

BAe Lightning

Lightning T.5 and F.6 (data for F.6)

Origin: English Electric Aviation (now British Aerospace), UK.

Type: Single-seat all-weather interceptor.

Engines: Two 15,680lb (7,112kg) thrust Rolls-Royce Avon 302 afterburning turbojets.

Dimensions: Span 34ft 10in (10.6m); length 53ft 3in (16.25m); height 19ft 7in (5.95m); wing area 380.1sq ft (35.31m^2).

Weights: Empty about 28,000lb (12,700kg); loaded 50,000lb (22,680kg).

Performance: Maximum speed 1,500mph (2,415km/h) at 40,000ft (12,200m); initial climb 50,000ft (15,240m)/min; service ceiling over 60,000ft (18,290m); range without overwing tanks 800 miles (1,290km).

Armament: Interchangeable packs for two all-attitude Red Top or stern-chase Firestreak guided missiles; option of two 30mm Aden cannon in forward part of belly tank; export versions up to 6,000lb (2,722kg) bombs or other offensive stores above and below wings.

History: First flight (P.1B) 4 April 1957; (first production F.1) 30 October 1959; (first F.6) 17 April 1964.

Users: UK (RAF).

Deployment: English Electric, later BAC and today BAe's Warton Division, built 338 Lightnings which, despite extreme disinterest by the RAF and political dislike by the Government (because it was a manned aircraft), were

eventually allowed to grow in power, fuel capacity and weapon capability. In the RAF, however, it has always been a pure local-defence interceptor, and even the definitive F.6 variant has no air/ground capability. Indeed, even the overwing ferry tanks are no longer fitted, restricting the aircraft to 1,200gal (5,455 litres), which would be consumed in six minutes in full afterburner. Primary armament of Red Tops remains fairly effective, and can be used from any firing angle including head-on. The two cannon in the front half of the belly tank are a good installation, causing no visible flash at night, and pilots have always undergone an intensive air/air gunnery course at an annual Armament Practice Camp at Akrotiri, Cyprus. No longer in service with RAF Germany, the Lightning remains an operational interceptor with Nos 5 and 11 Sqns, No 11 Group, Strike Command (No 11 Group is due to be merged into No 1 Group in 1984). The last F.3 single-seaters are now stored, together with about 40 Lightnings of various marks which in 1979-82 had been expected to form an additional air-defence squadron. The F.6 and a few T.5 two-seaters will now remain as local-defence interceptors until replaced by the Tornado F.2 in 1984-86.

Below: In this profile a Lightning F.6 of No 5 Sqn is depicted with wingless Red Top training missiles.

Foot of page: Lightnings no longer equip 19 Sqn (photo taken over BAe's Warton factory).

BAe Sea Harrier

Sea Harrier FRS.1

Origin: British Aerospace, UK.
Type: Multi-role STOVL naval combat aircraft.
Engine: One 21,500lb (9,752kg) thrust Rolls-Royce Pegasus 104 vectored-thrust turbofan.
Dimensions: Span 25ft 3in (7.7m); length 47ft 7in (14.5m); height 12ft 2in (3.71m); wing area 201.1sq ft (18.68m²).
Weights: Empty, not disclosed but about 12,250lb (5,557kg); maximum (non-VTOL) probably 25,000lb (11,340kg).
Performance: Maximum speed over 737mph (1,186km/h); typical lo attack speed 690mph (1,110km/h); hi intercept radius (3min combat plus reserves and vertical landing) 460 miles (750km); lo strike radius 288 miles (463km).
Armament: Normally fitted with two 30mm Aden Mk 4 each with 150 rounds; five hardpoints for max weapon load of 8,000lb (3,630kg) including Sea Eagle or Harpoon ASMs, Sidewinder AAMs and very wide range of other stores.
History: First flight 20 August 1978; service delivery 18 June 1979; first squadron commissioned 19 September 1979.
User: UK (RN).

Deployment: Delayed for many years by successive bouts of indecision by the customer, the Sea Harrier at last got the go-ahead in May 1975, though even then the idea of seagoing fixed-wing airpower was still as taboo as RAF combat aircraft had been at the start of the Harrier programme. Gradually the proposed "through-deck cruiser" became openly spoken of as a carrier for this STOVL (short takeoff, vertical landing) aircraft which was most successfully developed from the Harrier chiefly by redesigning the forward fuselage. The deeper structure provides for a versatile and compact Ferranti Blue Fox radar, which folds 180° for shipboard stowage, and a new cockpit with the seat raised to provide space for a much-enhanced nav/attack/combat system, and give an all-round view. The Royal Navy purchased 24, plus a further 10, FRS.1s, the designation meaning 'fighter, recon, strike' (strike normally means nuclear, but the Fleet Air Arm has not confirmed this capability). In the NATO context the main task is air defence at all heights, normally with direction from surface vessels, either as DLI (deck-launched intercept) or CAP (combat air patrol). In the Falklands fighting, in which almost all the RN Sea Harriers (28 out of 32) took part, these aircraft repeatedly demonstrated their ability to fly six sorties a day in extremely severe weather, with maintenance by torchlight at night often in hail blizzards. Serviceability was consistently around 95 per cent each morning. CAPs were flown at 10,000ft (3km) at 290mph (463km/h), and within a few seconds it was possible to be closing on an enemy at 690mph just above the sea; 24 Argentine aircraft were destroyed by AIM-9L Sidewinders and seven by guns. In air-ground missions main stores were ▶

Above: A Sea Harrier FRS.1 of No 800 Sqn, with early Sidewinder AIM-9B missiles, photographed with HMS *Hermes* in 1981, after the squadron numbers had been altered to begin with figure 1.

Below: Appearance of one of the first Sea Harriers on the commissioning of No 800 Sqn at HMS *Heron* (RNAS Yeovilton) in April 1980. All markings were oversprayed in April 1982.

▶ 1,000lb (454kg) bombs, Paveway 'smart' bombs and BL.755 clusters. Many new techniques were demonstrated including 4,000-mile (6,440km) flights to land on ships (sometimes by pilots who had never landed on a ship) and operations from quickly added sheet laid on the top row of containers in a merchant ship.

From this harsh self-sufficient campaign it is a major step to the more sophisticated European environment of greater density and diversity of forces, and especially of emitters (though Sea Harriers did use jammer pods in the South Atlantic). The E-2C and other aircraft would normally be available for direction, and the Sea Harrier is envisaged as filling the fleet defensive band between ship-to-air missiles and long-range F-14s with Phoenix AAMs. Its ESM fit is more advanced than that of Harriers and is used as a primary aid to intercept emitting aircraft (or, it is expected, sea-skimming missiles). Pilots normally operate as individuals, flying any mission for which they are qualified. After the Falklands war 14 additional aircraft were ordered to replace losses from all causes (6) and increase establishment of the three combat squadrons (800, 801 and 809, normally embarked aboard *Invincible*, *Illustrious* and *Hermes* [later *Ark Royal*]) and the training unit 899 Sqn at Yeovilton.

Below: Another April 1980 picture showing the 'peace-time' appearance of the FRS.1 of Lt-Cdr T.J.H. Gedge, first CO of reformed 800 Sqn. It served in the Falklands, the CO then being Lt-Cdr Andrew Auld.

Right: A pre-Falklands vic made up of Sea Harriers from: 899 HQ squadron (leading), 801 Sqn (nearest camera) and 800 Sqn (aircraft 124). A new unit, No 809, was hastily formed and fought from *Hermes*.

BAe Vulcan

Vulcan B.2B, K.2

Origin: A. V. Roe and Hawker Siddeley Aviation (now BAe Manchester).
Type: Long-range bomber (K.2, tanker).
Engines: Four 20,000lb (9,072kg) thrust Rolls-Royce (Bristol) Olympus 301 turbojets.
Dimensions: Span 111ft 0in (33.38m); length (including probe) 105ft 6in (32.16m); height 27ft 2in (8.28m); wing area, 3,964sq ft (368m^2).
Weights: Empty, about 105,000lb (47,628kg); maximum loaded, not disclosed but about 250,000lb (113,400kg).
Performance: Maximum speed (high altitude) 645mph (1,038km/h); max cruising speed 625mph (1,006km/h); range with max bombload 4,600 miles (7,403km).
Armament: Normal bombload 21 standard 1,000lb (454kg) GP bombs; provision for carrying nuclear stores no longer used (in the South Atlantic all Vulcans carried Sidewinder self-defence missiles on underwing pylons, as well as ECM jammer pods, usually the obsolescent Westinghouse ALQ-101, and Shrike anti-radar missiles).
History: First flight 30 August 1952, (prototype B.2) 31 August 1957, (production B.2) 30 August 1958; final delivery 1964.
User: UK (RAF).

Deployment: In 1981 the beautifully engineered bat-winged Vulcan equipped No 230 OCU and six squadrons of RAF No 1 Group, Strike Command, as well as No 27 Sqn operating in the long-range maritime reconnaissance role, with multiple sensors and extra fuel replacing bombs. The former high-altitude nuclear bombers, which at one time carried the Blue Steel stand-off missile and were then expected to carry Skybolt missiles on wing pylons, had since 1963 operated in the low-level

Above: A halcyon study of a B.2 taken in mid-1960s when low-level operations were new (passive warning and TFR are both absent).

conventional role, assigned to SACEUR as part of the UK-based long-range interdiction force. Like the B-52 they relied heavily on advanced defensive as well as offensive avionics to penetrate hostile airspace safely. Squadrons were progressively withdrawn from 1981, pending re-equipment with Tornados, and at the start of the Falklands campaign few were left operational in four truncated squadrons. A small number were hastily dispatched to Wideawake (Ascension) from where, with multiple refuellings from Victors, they made the longest combat missions in history, round trips of over 7,960 miles (12,800km) mainly in night attacks on the Stanley runway. On each trip 21 bombs of 1,000lb were dropped. New probes had to be fitted and the un-maintained flight refuelling systems completely overhauled. Six Vulcans were hastily modified to carry inflight-refuelling hosereels in place of ECM gear, and these remain in the Strike Command tanker force. Unfortunately the SR.2 aircraft of 27 Sqn have been withdrawn, leaving a gap in NATO's oceanic surveillance. All remaining serviceable Vulcans were expected, in late 1982, to be retained combat-ready as insurance against further adventures in the South Atlantic.

Left: XM571 was one of the six aircraft modified to serve as an inflight-refuelling tanker, the HDU (hose-drum unit) replacing ECM.

Below: One of the last Vulcans still in service with 44 Sqn, though it was not one of the five modified to participate in Black Buck missions to the Falklands.

XL445

Boeing B-52 Stratofortress

B-52D, G and H

Origin: Boeing Airplane Company (from May 1961 The Boeing Company), USA.

Type: Heavy bomber and missile platform.

Engines: (D) eight 12,100lb (5,489kg) thrust P&WA J57-19W or 29W turbojets, (G) eight 13,750lb (6,237kg) thrust P&WA J57-43W or -43WB turbojets, (H) eight 17,000lb (7,711kg) thrust P&WA TF33-1 or -3 turbofans.

Dimensions: Span 185ft 0in (56.39m); length (D, and G/H as built) 157ft 7in (48.0m); (G/H modified) 160ft 11in (49.05m); height (D) 48ft 4½in (14.7m), (G/H) 40ft 8in (12.4m); wing area 4,000sq ft (371.6m²).

Weights: Empty (D) about 175,000lb (79,380kg), (G/H) about 195,000ib (88,450kg); loaded (D) about 470,000lb (213,200kg), (G) 505,000lb (229,000kg), (H) 505,000 at takeoff, inflight refuel to 566,000lb (256,738kg).

Performance: Maximum speed (true airspeed, clean), (D) 575mph (925km/h), (G/H) 595mph (957km/h); penetration speed at low altitude (all) about 405mph (652km/h, Mach 0.53); service ceiling (D) 45,000ft (13.7km), (G) 46,000ft (14.0km), (H) 47,000ft (14.3km); range (max fuel, no external bombs/missiles, optimum hi-alt cruise) (D) 7,370 miles (11,861km), (G) 8,406 miles (13,528km), (H) 10,130 miles (16,303km); takeoff run, (D) 11,100ft (3,383m), (G) 10,000ft (3,050m), (H) 9,500ft (2,895m).

Armament: (D) four 0.5in (12.7mm) guns in occupied tail turret, MD-9 system, plus 84 bombs of nominal 500lb (227kg) in bomb bay plus 24 of nominal 750lb (340kg) on wing pylons, total 60,000lb (27,215kg); (G) four 0.5in (12.7mm) guns in remote-control tail turret, ASG-15 system, plus 8 nuclear bombs or up to 20 SRAM, ALCM, Harpoon or MRASM, or mix (eight on internal dispenser plus 12 on wing pylons), (H) single 20mm six-barrel gun in remote-control tail turret, ASG-21 system, plus bombload as G (not yet equipped for ALCM, Harpoon or MRASM).

History: First flight 15 April 1952; later, see text.

User: USA (Air Force).　▶

Above: The first SAC squadron of B-52Gs to become operational with the AGM-86B cruise missile reached initial capability at Griffiss AFB in December 1982. Here the 12 externally carried missiles can be seen on their pylons. Internal carriage is not possible, but the bays are to be rebuilt later in the 1980s.

Left: Built in larger numbers (193) than any other version, the B-52G is the lead variant in the CMI (cruise-missile integration) programme. This aircraft has yet to be fitted with the costly OAS (offensive avionic system) and CMI pylons.

Below: Last of the earlier models with flexible fuel cells in the wings and a giant tailfin, the B-52D still wears the black livery applied during the Southeast Asia war.

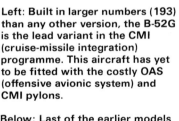

▶**Deployment:** The B-52 entered service with USAF Strategic Air Command (SAC) in August 1954 and became operational in June 1955. It was designed to drop small loads of nuclear weapons from the stratosphere, and was designed to extremely close limits in such factors as airframe weight in the expectancy it would be replaced by 1957-60. Today the B-52 is not only still in service but some will have to go on well into the 1990s, and its life is a thousand times tougher, carrying heavy loads of conventional ordnance and stand-off missiles, internally and externally, with all penetrations of hostile airspace at low altitude.

To fit them for their ongoing tasks all B-52s currently in the SAC inventory have been the subject of 16 extensive and expensive modification programmes, with eight yet to come, to prolong structure life and provide avionics and weapons adequate for the missions. About 80 B-52Ds remain in service, configured for large loads of conventional bombs, but the most important variants are the newest. The B-52G (170 remain of 193 built) has since 1981 been converted to carry not only the supersonic SRAM (see companion volume, *Airborne Missiles*) but also the long-range ALCM cruise missile. SRAM was already carried by the fan-engined B-52H (about 90 remain of 102). B-52s have secondary tasks which include sea surveillance and minelaying, and in spring 1983 a B-52G was to begin tests with Harpoon anti-ship missiles. In the sea-control mission a missile-armed B-52G could fly 2,000 miles (3,220km) from a coastal base, loiter for 2h and return without refuelling. B-52s have even launched tactical weapons such as the GBU-15 smart attack missile, and another plan is to carry 12 Assault Breaker anti-armour missiles (using the Patriot SAM airframe) on the wing pylons, together with the associated Pave Mover radar. Yet another weapon is MRASM, in AGM-109H form in the anti-runway mission. Thus the B-52 could play a major role at the tactical level in any future conflict in Europe.

Right: Maintenance on the B-52s (called Buffs, meaning Big Ugly Fat Fellas) is helped by most parts being newer than the B-52.

Below: A surviving B-52D doing free-fall bombing practice on a low-level range (probably at Guam, in the Pacific).

Dassault-Breguet Mirage III and 5

Mirage III and 5

Origin: Avions Marcel Dassault/Breguet Aviation, France (actual manufacture dispersed through French and Belgian industry).

Type: Single-seat or two-seat interceptor, tactical strike, trainer or reconnaissance aircraft (depending on sub-type).

Engine: (IIIC) 13,225lb (6,000kg) thrust (maximum afterburner) SNECMA Atar 9B turbojet; (most other III and some 5) 13,670lb (6,200kg) Atar 9C.

Dimensions: Span 27ft (8.22m); length (excl probe) (IIIC) 48ft 5in (14.75m), (IIIE) 49ft 3½in (15.03m), (5) 51ft 0¼in (15.55m); height 13ft 11½in (4.25m); wing area 375sq ft (35.0m²).

Weights: Empty (IIIC) 13,570lb (6,156kg); (IIIE) 15.540lb (7,050kg); (IIIR) 14,550lb (6,600kg); (IIIB) 13,820lb (6,270kg); (5) 14,550lb (6,600kg); loaded (IIIC) 19,700lb (8,936kg); (IIIE, IIIR, 5) 29,760lb (13,500kg); (IIIB) 26,455lb (12,000kg).

Performance: Maximum speed (all models, clean) 863mph (1,390km/h) (Mach 1.14) at sea level, 1,460mph (2,350km/h) (Mach 2.2) at altitude; initial climb, over 16,400ft (5,000m)/min (time to 36,090ft 11,000m, 3 ▶

Above: Though limited in range and mission equipment (both volume and available weight) the Mirage IIIR has for 20 years been the sole tac-recon aircraft of the Armée de l'Air. The 33ᵉ Escadre is now converting to the Mirage F1.CR.

Above: One of the 20 Mirage 5F attack aircraft (originally built and paid for by Israel) which equip EC3/13 Auvergne at Colmar. This version has a longer and slimmer nose than the Mirage IIIs.

Left: Though amazingly maladjusted to the need, in having very fast takeoff and landing and poor all-weather avionics, the Mirage 5BA, of the FAB (Belgian air force) has long enjoyed some of the best inbuilt ECM of any tactical aircraft in NATO. Loral, the supplier, is likely to equip many F-16s.

min); service ceiling (Mach 1.8) 55,775ft (17,000m); range (clean) at altitude about 1,000 miles (1,610km); combat radius in attack mission with two bombs and tanks (hi-altitude) 745 miles (1,200km); ferry range with three external tanks, 2,485 miles (4,000km).

Armament: Two 30mm DEFA 5-52 cannon, each with 125 rounds (normally fitted to all versions except when IIIC carries rocket-boost pack); three 1,000lb (454kg) external pylons for bombs, missiles or tanks (Mirage 5, seven external pylons with maximum capacity of 9,260lb, 4,200kg).

History: First flight (prototype Mirage III-001) 17 November 1956; (production IIIC) 9 October 1960; (prototype 5) 19 May 1967; (Belgian-assembled 5BA) May 1970.

Users: (III) France, Spain; (5), Belgium, France.

Deployment: When the French Armée de l'Air adopted the Mirage III in 1957 it bought a world pioneer Mach 2 combat aircraft with quite good interception capability at all altitudes, especially at great heights where the optional SEP liquid rocket pack (used by French squadrons) gave exceptional speed and agility. Dassault designed the Mirage III to be able to operate from rough front-line airstrips, but its high landing speed of (minimum) 180mph (290km/h) and consequent long field length precludes operation from all except smooth surfaces with a length of some 6,600ft (2km). The Mirage IIIC, the first production version, is still in

Right: Now at last being replaced by the Mirage 2000, the Armée de l'Air's Mirage IIIC interceptors can be distinguished by twin-eyelid engine nozzle, and the old R 530 missile.

Above: Though fairly simple and cheap, the Mirage 5BA has suffered high attrition with the Force Aérienne Belge, and has never been able to fly the necessary all-weather attack missions.

service with two squadrons of EC 10 at Creil and with EC 2/2, the OCU, but all will have been withdrawn by spring 1983, replacements being the Mirage F1.C and F1.B. Much more important, the IIIE has a longer fuselage and more comprehensive avionics for attack missions. It equips two squadrons of EC2 at Dijon, two squadrons of EC 4 at Luxeuil (carrying the AN 52 15-kiloton tactical nuclear bomb) and one squadron of EC 13 at Colmar. The other two EC 13 squadrons fly the Mirage 5F, a simple attack aircraft which also equips Nos 1 and 2 Sqns of the Belgian AF plus the Belgian Mirage OCU, No 8 Sqn. The Mirage IIIR recon aircraft equips the French ER 33 at Strasbourg (from 1983 to convert to the F1.R). Spain's EdA flies the IIIEE in the 11th Ala (wing) Nos 111 and 112 Escuadróns at Manises. These will be the first units to re-equip with the F/A-18A. In a primitive limited-war environment the early delta Mirages would be quite effective, but they lack the combination of endurance, weapon load and avionics needed for the European environment. Belgium's Mirage 5BA does have Loral II internal ECM and a good weapon load, but lacks all-weather nav/attack systems.

Left: Spain's Ejercito del Aire (air force) is one of the larger users of early delta Mirages, as well as even larger numbers of the F1.C series. This profile illustrates a IIIEE (known as a C-11) which flies with Esc 112 at Manises near Valencia on the east coast of mainland Spain. Their primary role is interception. Replacement is the F/A-18A.

Dassault-Breguet Mirage F1

Mirage F1.C

Origin: Avions Marcel Dassault/Breguet Aviation, France, in partnership with Aérospatiale, SABCA, Belgium, and CASA, Spain.

Type: Single-seat multimission fighter; (E) all-weather strike, (R) recon, (B) dual trainer.

Engine: 15,873lb (7,200kg) thrust (maximum afterburner) SNECMA Atar 9K-50 augmented turbojet.

Dimensions: Span 27ft 6¾in (8.4m); length (F1.C) 49ft 2½in (15m); (F1.E) 50ft 11in (15.53m); height (F1.C) 14ft 9in (4.5m), (F1.E) 14ft 10½in (4.56m); wing area 269.1sq ft (25.0m²).

Weights: Empty (F1.C) 16,314lb (7,400kg); (F1.E) 17,857lb (8,100kg); loaded (clean) (F1.C) 24,030lb (10,900kg), (F1.E) 25,450lb (11,540kg); (maximum) (F1.C) 32,850lb (14,900kg); (F1.E) 33,510lb (15,200kg).

Performance: Maximum speed (clean, both versions) 915mph (1,472km/h) (Mach 1.2) at sea level, 1,450mph (2,335km/h) (Mach 2.2) at altitude (with modification to cockpit transparency and airframe leading edges F1.E capable of 2.5); rate of climb (sustained to Mach 2 at 33,000ft) (F1.C) 41,930—47,835ft (12,780—14,580m)/min, (F1E) above 59,000ft (18,000m)/min; service ceiling (F1.C) 65,600ft (20,000m), (F1.E) 69,750ft (21,250m); range with maximum weapons (hi-lo-hi) (F1.C) 560 miles (900km), (F1.E) 621 miles (1,000km); ferry range (F1.C) 2,050 miles (3,300km), (F1.E) 2,340 miles (3,765km).

Armament: (Both versions), two 30mm DEFA 5-53 cannon, each with 135 rounds; five pylons, rated at 4,500lb (2,000kg) on centreline, 2,800lb ▶

Above: A Mirage F1.C of the 12 Escadre fully armed with the excellent combination of two Super 530s for long range or interception of very low or very high targets, plus two Magics on the wing tips.

Below: EC 5, normally based at Orange in southern France, is the only operator of the F1.C-200, equipped with a fixed inflight-refuelling probe. Unit is 2/5 'Ile de France'; the store is the finned tank.

▶ (1,350kg) inners and 1,100lb (500kg) outers; launch rails on tips rated at 280lb (120kg) for air-to-air missiles; total weapon load 8,820lb (4,000kg). Typical air combat weapons, two Matra 550 Magic for close combat, one/two Matra Super 530 for long-range homing. Optional reconnaissance pod containing cameras, SAT Cyclope infrared linescan and EMI side-looking radar.

History: First flight (F1-01) 23 December 1966; (production F1.C) 15 February 1973; (F1.B trainer) 26 May 1976; service delivery (F1.C) 14 March 1973.

Users: France, Greece, Spain.

Deployment: First flown in 1966, the F1 series stemmed from the much larger F2, scaled down to have a single Atar similar to that in earlier Mirages though of the most powerful sub-type (the same 9K-50 engine is used in some non-NATO delta Mirages). The F1 has a wing much smaller than the deltas but so much more efficient that the F1 has much shorter field length, slower landing, and (with 40 per cent greater internal fuel) three times the supersonic endurance, or twice the tactical radius at low levels, with superior all-round manoeuvrability. With long-stroke twin-wheel main gears and a landing speed of 143mph (230km/h) the F1 is also more genuinely able to use short unpaved airstrips. The Armée de l'Air achieved operational capability with the F1.C at Reims (30e Escadre), followed by 5e Escadre at Orange (whose three squadrons include 25 of the F1.C-200 type with permanent FR probes to permit non-stop deployment to Djibouti, 3,100 miles, 5,000km, and similar distant points) and EC 12 at Cambrai. Equipped with Cyrano IV radar and the excellent combination of Magic and Super 530 AAMs, the F1.C is one of the best interceptors in Western Europe. The Armée de l'Air's 225 F1s include 30 F1.R recon aircraft which from 1983 have been replacing IIIRs with ER 33. Greece uses the F1.CG in 334 Mire at Tanagra in the interception role. Spain's EdA flies 44 F1.CE interceptors with Esc 141 and 142 at Los Llanos and 22 F1.EEs in the strike (non-nuclear) role at Gando (Canaries) with Esc 462. The F1 family were in 1983 all fully effective modern aircraft with good all-round capability in all weather. French F1 aircraft can carry the Thomson-CSF Remora self-protection jammer pod and the large Caiman offensive jammer when operating in the dedicated EW role.

Below: Known as the C14 to the Ejercito del Aire (Spanish AF) the Mirage F1.CE is shown in markings of Escuadron 141, at Los Llanos.

Below: Newest fighter of the Elliniki Aeroporia (Greek AF) is the F1.CG seen here in the markings of 114 Wing.

Above: This F1.C of Armée de
l'Air EC 1/5 'Vendee' is armed
with two old R 530 AAMs far
inferior to today's Super 530.

Dassault-Breguet Mirage 2000

Mirage 2000, 2000B and 2000N

Origin: Avions Marcel Dassault/Breguet Aviation, France.

Type: Multi-role fighter with emphasis on interception and air superiority combat.

Engine: One SNECMA M53-5 afterburning by-pass turbojet (low-ratio turbofan) with maximum thrust of 12,350lb (5,602kg) dry and 19,840lb (9,000kg) with afterburner.

Dimensions: Span 29ft 6in (9.0m); length (2000) 47ft 1in (14.35m), (2000B) 47ft 9in (14.55m); height 17ft 6in (5.3m); wing area 441sq ft (41m²).

Weights: Empty 16,315lb (7,400kg); normal takeoff, air-intercept mission 33,000lb (14,969kg); maximum 36,375lb (16,500kg).

Performance: Maximum continuous speed at 36,000ft (11,000m) Mach 2.2, 1,320mph (2,124km/h); maximum attack speed at low level 690mph (1,110km/h); range with two tanks, over 1,118 miles (1,800km).

Armament: Two 30mm DEFA 5-53 cannon; normal air-intercept load two Matra Super 530 and two Matra 550 Magic air-to-air missiles; intention is to develop ground-attack version with maximum overload of 13,225lb (6,000kg) of weapons and/or tanks and ECM pods on nine external hardpoints.

History: Announcement of project December 1975; first flight 10 March 1978; production delivery, probably mid 1983.

User: France. ▶

Above: Takeoff at an air display by Mirage 2000 prototype No 04 carrying dummy Magics, a tank and six Matra Beluga bomblet dispensers (seven of the latter can in fact be carried).

Below: The 2000 B01, the first tandem dual trainer prototype, first flew on 11 October 1980. Several production 2000Bs are included in the 73 aircraft ordered for the Armée de l'Air.

▶ **Deployment:** After agonizing periods of indecision this small delta was chosen by Dassault and the Armée de l'Air in December 1975, and the larger twin-engined ACF (Avion de Combat Futur), for which the M53 engine had been designed, was terminated. In most respects the Mirage 2000 is a modern and potentially very agile aircraft, well suited to the air-combat role and equipped with an excellent mix of guns, close-range Magic AAMs and medium-range Super 530 AAMs. Structurally, aero-dynamically and in its fly-by-wire flight controls providing artificial stability as well as trajectory control the 2000 is well up to the current state of the art, and its only fundamental difficulty appears to be its price (export customers having quoted various prices in excess of US$38 million). Where the 2000 shows up less well are in the basic questions of propulsion and avionics, the engine being less-powerful than the ideal, relatively heavy, and with a high fuel consumption (except on the very brief occasions when a dash is made at over Mach 2). It is hoped that a more powerful P2 version

Below: A new profile of a production Mirage 2000 for the Armée de l'Air. The markings shown are those of EC 10, which is overdue for replacing its Mirage IIICs used in the interception role from Creil, north of Paris.

Foot of page: Whatever other problems may affect both programmes, the Mirage 2000 and (beyond) the Super Mirage 4000 are aesthetically very attractive aircraft. The first prototypes of each type are here depicted.

will be developed. The RDI pulse-doppler radar has been delayed even more than the rest of the aircraft, and the earlier RDM (originally planned only for export customers) must be fitted to all production aircraft delivered before late 1985. First deliveries, originally expected in 1981, will take place in 1983 to EC 2 at Dijon, replacing the Mirage IIIE in the attack role (in which the large wing area gives severe gust response even at the modest 690mph speed). The Mirage 2000 can carry a formidable bombload, but its qualities fit it much better to the interception mission, in which it is an excellent aircraft in a totally different class from earlier delta Mirages. The Armée de l'Air ordered four in 1979 followed by three annual increments of 22, the intention being that these would operate in the air-defence role. Dassault hopes to sell 200 in this role, plus as many again for reconnaissance and strike, but Armée de l'Air decisions are proving very difficult.

The Mirage 4000, an enlarged delta with two M53 engines, has been produced at company expense. It had not found a buyer in early 1983.

Dassault Mirage IVA

Mirage IVA

Origin: Avions Marcel Dassault (now AMD/BA), France.
Type: Supersonic bomber, multisensor reconnaissance and 'buddy' refuelling tanker.
Engines: two 15,432lb (7,000kg) thrust SNECMA Atar 9K afterburning turbojets.
Dimensions: Span 38ft 10½in (11.85m); length 77ft 1in (23.5m); height 17ft 8½in (5.40m); wing area 840sq ft (78.0m²).
Weights: Empty 32,820lb (14,887kg); maximum 73,800lb (33,475kg).
Performance: Maximum speed (one recessed bomb, 40,000ft/13,125m, brief dash) 1,454mph (2,340km/h); low-level penetration speed 690mph (1,110km/h); mission radius (one recessed bomb, two tanks, one unspecified supersonic dash period) 770 miles (1,240km).
Armament: One 60-kilotonne free-fall nuclear bomb recessed under fuselage; alternatively up to 16,000lb (7,257kg) of conventional stores on body/wing pylons. Provision for two tanks (one can be a buddy hosereel pack) and ECM pods; later ASMP, see text.
History: First flight 17 June 1959; first production aircraft 7 December 1963; final delivery 1967.
User: France.

Deployment: The creation of a French nuclear deterrent (*Force de Dissuasion*) involved silo-based missiles, submarine-based missiles and recallable manned bombers. The bold decision was taken, for budgetary reasons, to use a supersonic bomber too small to fly typical round-trip missions unaided. Instead the Mirage IVA, tailored around a pair of engines basically similar to those used in Mirage fighters, either takes off with a partner of the same type serving as the tanker, to replenish the bomber on its outward journey (the Boeing C-135F is also used for the same purpose),

Below: Almost all simulated missions with the Mirage IVA are flown at the lowest possible level, rising to take on fuel.

Above: It is significant that, while USAF withdrew the much longer-ranged B-58 on cost grounds, Mirage IVAs soldier on.

or it recovers to what is hoped to be friendly or neutral territory after dropping its bomb. Dassault built 62 production aircraft, of which 47 are in the active inventory, 24 of these being at readiness in six four-aircraft Escadrons (each Esc normally comprising one bomber and one tanker, both with C-135F support). The six bases are Mont de Marsan, St Dizier, Cazaux, Orange, Avord and Luxeuil, and additional dispersal strips are available for time of crisis. A further 12 Mirage IVAs are equipped for strategic reconnaissance; it is not known if they can fly this mission effectively at low level, like the bombers. From 1986 (more likely 1987) the long-range ASMP stand-off missile is expected to be carried by the IVA, one under each wing probably in addition to tanks.

Dassault-Breguet Super Etendard

Super Etendard

Origin: Avions Marcel Dassault/Breguet Aviation, France.
Type: Single-seat carrier strike fighter.
Engine: 11,265lb (5,110kg) thrust SNECMA Atar 8K-50 turbojet.
Dimensions: Span 31ft 5¾in (9.6m); length 46ft 11½in (14.31m); height 12ft 8in (3.85m); wing area 305.7sq ft (28.4m²).
Weights: Empty 14,220lb (6,450kg); loaded 25,350lb (11,500kg).
Performance: Maximum speed 745mph (1,200km/h) at sea level, Mach 1 at altitude; initial climb 24,600ft (7,500m)/min; service ceiling 45,000ft (13,700m); radius (hi-lo-hi, one AM 39, one tank) 403 miles (650km).
Armament: Two 30mm DEFA cannon, each with 125 rounds; five pylons for weapon load with full internal fuel of 4,630lb (2,100kg); one AM 39 Exocet can be carried (right wing) with one tank (left).
History: First flight (converted Etendard) 28 October 1974; first delivery, late 1977.
User: France (Aéronavale).   ▶

Above: With the abandonment of fixed-wing seagoing airpower by Britain—a decision bitterly regretted in the spring of 1982— France is the only carrier-equipped country in Western Europe, with two (probably nuclear) carriers planned. Aircraft here are Super Etendards (and one Etendard IVM).

Above: The first Dassault-Breguet Super Etendard pictured on flight test. The type entered service with the Aéronavale in June 1978, and all were delivered by the end of 1982. Though classed as a fighter the flight performance is inadequate for success in this role.

Below: Not replaced by the Super Etendard, the Etendard IVP still serves in the photo-reconnaissance role with Flottille 16F at Landivisiau. The belly camera pack may be replaced by a tank or by a 'buddy' inflight-refuelling hosereel pod.

▶Deployment: Dassault originally delivered 69 Etendard IVM carrier-based attack aircraft to the French Aéronavale in 1962-64, together with 21 of the IVP photographic-recon version. A naval Jaguar was produced and tested, but Dassault managed to get this rejected as an Etendard replacement by its own Super Etendard, with the advantage of some commonality with the earlier machine. Though called a strike fighter the Super Etendard has little air-combat capability against enemy high-performance aircraft and is used almost wholly in an air/surface role. Equipment includes an Agave multi-mode radar which is fully adequate for most attacks on surface ships, a Sagem (Kearfott licence) inertial nav/attack system, BF radar warning system and DB-3141 ECM jammer pod. Free-fall bombs of 250 and 400kg sizes can be carried, but the chief anti-ship weapon is the AM 39 Exocet (Super Etendards of the Argentine navy destroyed HMS *Sheffield* and the *Atlantic Conveyor* with AM 39s, though the former ship succumbed to a fire started by the missile's sustainer motor, the warhead failing to detonate). The Aéronavale planned to buy 100 Super Etendards but inflation reduced the total to 71 in 1978-82. These equip Flottilles 11F and 14F at Landivisiau, 17F at Hyères and 12F at Landivisiau, the latter in the interception mission replacing the Mach 2 Crusader. The IVP remains in use, but a reconnaissance version of the Super has long been projected. Super Etendard flottilles go to sea aboard the small and aged *Clémenceau* and *Foch,* to replace which two 32,000-tonne nuclear carriers are planned for the end of the century.

Below: Third Super Etendard pictured on carrier trials in the Mediterranean; later trials were in heavy seas in the Atlantic.

Below: Primary anti-ship armament of the Super Etendard is a single AM 39 Exocet, balanced by a tank under the left wing (trials with No 1 prototype).

Above: Steam-catapult launch of the eighth Super Etendard,
carrying the usual underwing tanks. Note the tailplane angle.

Dassault-Breguet/Dornier Alpha Jet

Alpha Jet

Origin: Jointly Dassault-Breguet, France, and Dornier GmbH, W Germany, with assembly at each company.

Type: two-seat trainer and light strike/reconnaissance aircraft.

Engines: two 2,976lb (1,350kg) thrust SNECMA/Turboméca Larzac 04 turbofans.

Dimensions: Span 29ft 10¾in (9.11m); length (excluding any probe) 40ft 3¾in (12.29m); height 13ft 9in (4.2m); wing area 188.4sq ft (17.5m²).

Weights: (Trainer) empty 7,374lb (3,345kg); loaded (clean) 11,023lb (5,000kg) (max) 16,535lb (7,500kg).

Performance: (Clean) maximum speed 576mph (927km/h) at sea level, 560mph (900km/h) (Mach 0.85) at altitude; climb to 39,370ft (12,000m), less than 10 minutes; service ceiling 48,000ft (14,630m); typical mission endurance 2hr 30min; ferry range with two external tanks 1,827 miles (2,940km).

Armament: Optional for weapon training or combat missions, detachable belly fairing housing one 30mm DEFA or 27mm Mauser cannon, with 125 rounds; same centreline hardpoint and either one or two under each wing (to maximum of five) can be provided with pylons for maximum external load of 5,511lb (2,500kg), made up of tanks, weapons, reconnaissance pod, ECM or other devices.

History: First flight 26 October 1973; first production delivery late 1978.

Users: Belgium, France, W Germany. ▶

Above: Most early deliveries of Alpha Jet trainers (then called the Alpha Jet E) went to the 'Christian Martel' GE 314 wing at Tours St Symphorien, which eventually received more than 60.

Left: Belgian industry shared in manufacture of both the 33 FAB Alpha Jets and their Larzac 04 engines; this was the first.

Left: Almost all the early deliveries to the Armée de l'Air went to GE (Groupement Ecole) 314, named for Christian Martel, at Tours, which received 65. The next 45 when went to EC 8 at Cazaux (replacing Mystére IVs) and the final 65 went to GE 313. Some were sidetracked for the Patrouille de France.

▶ **Deployment:** Realisation that the Jaguar was too capable and costly to be a standard basic trainer led to the Armée de l'Air issuing a requirement for a new trainer in 1967. The chosen design was to be capable of use in the light ground attack role, in which the Luftwaffe had a parallel need for an aircraft. On 22 July 1969 the two governments agreed to a common specification, and deliveries of the Alpha Jet E (École, school) began in autumn 1978. This model serves with the Armée de l'Air (200 total) to equip the entire Groupement-École 314 'Christian Martel' at Tours, the Patrouille de France aerobatic team at Salon, the Centre d'Entrainement au Vol Sans Visibilité and the 8e Escadre de Transformation at Cazaux. It is also used (33 supplied) by Belgium's 7, 9 and 11 Sqns at St Truiden (St Trond). All these are pure training or display units, but the Federal German Luftwaffe uses a different version in the close-support and reconnaissance roles. The Alpha Jet A (Appui, support) has the Mauser gun, a pointed nose with pitot probe (aircraft length 43ft 5in, 13.23m) and MBB-built Stencel seats instead of Martin-Baker. A total of 153 was supplied to three fighter/bomber wings: JaboG 49 at Fürstenfeldbruck, JaboG 43 at Oldenburg and JaboG 41 at Husum, each with 51 aircraft on strength. They are austerely equipped for attack missions in the European environment, though navigation systems are good and a HUD (head-up display) is provided. The LaCroix BOZ-10 chaff pod has been developed jointly by France and Germany and is expected to appear with these JaboGs. In the recon role a Super Cyclope pod can be carried with optical cameras, IR linescan and a decoy launcher. Combat missions are expected to be strongly supported by Awacs (E-3A Sentry) coverage to make up for deficiencies in the Alpha Jet's defensive avionics. The Luftwaffe has 18 Alpha Jets in the weapon-training role at Beja, Portugal, the German total being 175.

Right: In many respects the Alpha Jet close-support version (originally called Alpha Jet A) differs from the French type. They are not trainers but are tasked with light attack and reconnaissance.

Above: A production trainer of l'Armée de l'Air with gear down and airbrakes open. Dassault-Breguet/Dornier have now built single examples of the NGEA attack version and a research machine with supercritical wing.

Left: The first prototype, demonstrating its ability to operate from unpaved surfaces. Development ran two years behind schedule.

Fairchild Republic A-10 Thunderbolt II

A-10A, A-10/T, A-10/NAW

Origin: Fairchild Republic Company, USA.

Type: Close-support attack aircraft.

Engines: Two 9,065lb (4,112kg) thrust General Electric TF34-100 turbofans.

Dimensions: Span 57ft 6in (17.53m); length 53ft 4in (16.26m); height (regular) 14ft 8in (4.47m); (NAW) 15ft 4in (4.67m); wing area 506sq ft (47m²).

Weights: Empty 21,519lb (9,761kg), forward airstrip weight (no fuel but four Mk 82 bombs and 750 rounds) 32,730lb (14,846kg), maximum 50,000lb (22,680kg), operating weight empty, 24,918lb (11,302kg), (NAW) 28,630lb (12,986kg).

Performance: Maximum speed, (max weight, A-10A) 423mph (681km/h), (NAW) 420mph (676km/h); cruising speed at sea level (both) 345mph (555km/h), stabilized speed below 8,000ft (2,440m) in 45° dive at weight 35,125lb (15,932kg)299mph (481km/h); maximum climb at basic design weight of 31,790lb (14,420kg), 6,000ft (1,828m)/min, service ceiling, not stated; takeoff run to 50ft (15m) at maximum weight, 4,000ft (1,220m); operating radius in CAS mission with 1.8 hour loiter and reserves, 288 miles (463km); radius for single deep strike penetration, 620 miles (1,000km); ferry range with allowances, 2,542 miles (4,091km).

Armament: One GAU-8/A Avenger 30mm seven-barrel gun with 1,174 rounds, total external ordnance load of 16,000lb (7,257kg) hung on 11 pylons, three side-by-side on body and four under each wing; several hundred combinations of stores up to individual weight of 5,000lb (2,268kg) with maximum total weight 14,638lb (6,640kg) with full internal fuel.

History: First flight (YA-10A) 10 May 1972, (production A-10A) 21 October 1975, (NAW) 4 May 1979.

▶

Above: Formation of A-10As serving with the Connecticut ANG (103 Tac Fighter Group, from Bradley Field).

Below: Fairchild have funded this NAW (night and adverse weather) two-seater, which appears much needed.

►**Deployment:** The concept of a close-support aircraft built around a gun of tremendous power, for use especially against armour and other hard-skinned targets, arose from the Co-In and light attack studies of the early 1960s. The AX programme was launched in 1967, and Fairchild Republic beat Northrop in the fly-off evaluation of the two best designs. From the start the planned force was to be large, initially set at 733 aircraft. The whole point of the A-10A was to be its firepower and immediate lethality against ground targets, and as far as possible it was made to withstand ground fire up to about 20mm calibre. Systems are duplicated and redundant, engines are high at the rear offering minimal infra-red signature and the aircraft can fly with one complete engine pod, half the tail and various other parts inoperative or shot away, and then land without further damage on its retracted wheels. The avionic fit was officially described as austere, and though adequate for a sunny day has never sufficed for accurate navigation and weapon delivery in the weather of northern Europe. The Pave Penny laser tracker has been an option from the first aircraft, but this merely senses ground targets already illuminated by a friendly laser. To provide proper sensors Fairchild Republic flew a two-seat A-10/NAW (night/adverse weather) prototype with Westinghouse multimode radar, Ferranti laser, Flir

(forward-looking infra-red) and GE low-light TV. It has not been put into production, but at least 30 of the 1981 increment of 60 A-10As are of the two-seat A-10/T combat-ready trainer variety and these could have night and all-weather sensors if a decision was taken. In any case the Martin Marietta Lantirn (low-altitude nav targeting IR for night) pods are expected eventually to be fitted to most A-10As, though cost escalation has placed Lantirn in jeopardy (late 1982). As this was written, 550 aircraft had been delivered to units of TAC and the ANG, as well as to the 81st TFW based at RAF Woodbridge and Bentwaters in England, and the 601 TCW at Sembach, Germany. Forward operating locations in Germany are routinely used. The A-10A has amply demonstrated good reliability, lethality and the ability to use many weapons, but many have crashed simply by hitting the ground, the aircraft being fully serviceable. To make up for high attrition the total has been increased to 825, but in late 1982 Congress terminated production at close to the original level.

Below: The tail code is difficult to read in this fine portrait but appears to be DM, signifying 355th Tac Fighter Wing from Davis-Monthan AFB. White AGM-65A Mavericks spoil the camouflage.

General Dynamics F-16 Fighting Falcon

F-16A, B, C and D

Origin: General Dynamics, Fort Worth, USA.

Type: (A,C): Multi-role fighter, (B,D) operational fighter/trainer.

Engine: One 23,840lb (10,814kg) thrust Pratt & Whitney F100-200 after-burning turbofan.

Dimensions: Span 31ft 0in (9.449m) (32ft 10in/10.1m over missile fins), length (both versions, excl probe) 47ft 7in (14.52m); wing area 300.0 sq ft (27.87m²).

Weights: Empty (A) 15,137lb (6,866kg), (B) 15,778lb (7,157kg); loaded (AAMs only) (A) 23,357lb (10,594kg), (B) 22,814lb (10,348kg), (max external load) (both) 35,400lb (16,057kg), (Block 25 on) 37,500lb (17,010kg).

Performance: Maximum speed (both, AAMs only) 1,350mph (2,173km/h, Mach 2.05) at 40,000ft (12.19km); maximum at SL, 915mph (1,472km/h, Mach 1.2), initial climb (AAMs only) 50,000ft (15.24km)/min; service ceiling, over 50,000ft (15.24km); tactical radius (A, six Mk 82, internal fuel, Hi-Lo-Hi) 340 miles (547km); ferry range, 2,415 miles (3,890km).

Armament: One M61A-1 20mm gun with 500/515 rounds, centreline pylon for 250gal (1,136lit) drop tank or 2,200lb (998kg) bomb, inboard wing pylons for 4,500lb (2,041kg) each, middle wing pylons for 3,500lb (1,587kg) each, outer wing pylons for 700lb (318kg) each (being uprated under MSIP-1 to 3,500lb), wingtip pylons for 425lb (193kg), all ratings being at 9g. Normal maximum load 11,950lb (5,420kg) for 9g, 20,450lb (9,276kg) at reduced load factor.

History: First flight (YF) 20 January 1974, (production F-16A) 7 August 1978; service delivery (A) 17 August 1978.

Users: Belgium, Denmark, Netherlands, Norway, USA (Air Force). ▶

Left: By the time this book appears the USAF may have chosen its advanced attack aircraft. One candidate is the F-16E (F-16XL), the first prototype of which is seen level bombing with 12 x 1,000lb.

Above: First meeting in 1979 of F-16Bs assembled in Europe for the four European NATO air force customers: front to rear, Denmark, Norway, Belgium and the Netherlands. Norway has tail parachute installation.

▶ **Deployment:** Built as a demonstrator of LWF (Light Weight Fighter) technology in 1974, very much in the face of official disinterest by the USAF (which was totally committed to the F-15 and could see no point in supporting a supposed inferior aircraft), the General Dynamics Model 401 was a design of unalloyed brilliance which, after a slight increase in size and judicious revision of the aerodynamics and fly-by-wire flight controls, was accepted by the USAF as the F-16A. Unexpectedly, and mainly because it was as well as the F-15, not instead of, the USAF bought first 650 and then committed itself to 1,388, not only outstripping the F-15 programme but representing a growth in real capability despite the ravages of inflation and cheese-pared budgets. In June 1975 the same aircraft was selected by the four NATO nations mentioned above, to replace the F-104 in both fighter and attack roles. General Dynamics not only made the production F-16A the most agile fighter in the sky but also gave it the capability to carry a fantastic bombload and deliver it with unprecedented accuracy. In its first participation in a numerically scored inter-service competition the F-16A demolished all opposition. At RAF Lossiemouth in June 1981 a team from the 388th TFW, from Hill AFB, Utah, scored 86-0 in air combat (the aggregate of rival teams was 42 losses and 1 kill); the F-16 unit scored far better than all others against Rapier SAM threats, was the only team to hit all assigned surface targets, and beat all comers in quick turnround between missions, finally setting the record score of 7,831 points out of 8,000 (an RAF Jaguar unit came second with 6,401). This vividly illustrates the tremendous all-round capability of even the initial F-16A, whose tandem dual partner the F-16B has roughly 17 per cent less internal fuel but retains full avionics and weapons capability. ▶

Above: This photo was clearly taken at the same occasion as that on previous page. The two-seater, which accounts for 17 per cent of the buy by these four air forces so far, is a fully combat-ready aircraft with about 17 per cent less internal fuel than the single-seater. A Wild Weasel F-16 would have two seats.

Right: One of the early F-16B two-seaters at the 388th TFW at Hill AFB was painted in Charcoal Lizard camouflage. It was unpopular.

Above: Two of the 1978-funded F-16As going round a loop. Virtually every pilot who has flown the F-16 says it is a new and exciting experience.

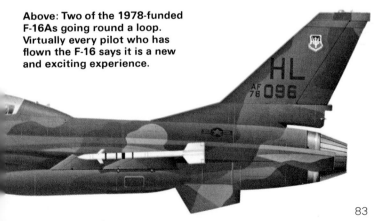

Above: Breaking away from its companion, an F-16A of the 8th
Tac Fighter Wing opens its airbrakes between the engine nozzle
and the slab tailplanes (which in current production are larger
than the tailplanes of these F-16s). The 8th TFW is based at Kunsan
AB, South Korea, and the badge on the fin is that of PacAf. The
famed Wolfpack name is perpetuated by the tail code and the
wolf's head on the fuselage.

Below: An F-16A Fighting Falcon of the Netherlands KLu, with the badge of No 306 Sqn (based at Leeuwarden) on its fin. Camouflage (and for Denmark and Belgium) is the same as for the USAF.

▶ When the four European countries selected the F-16 they insisted on substantial industrial offsets, and with remarkable speed a multinational manufacturing programme was set up to build production aircraft. All major aircraft, engine, avionics and accessory firms in the four European countries participate and there are assembly lines in Belgium (SABCA/SONACA) and the Netherlands (Fokker) as well as at Fort Worth. Though this has put up the costs, and still not achieved the potential output of which Fort Worth alone would be capable if working at maximum rate, the multinational programme has worked quite well and by late 1982 had delivered over 1,000 aircraft. By far the largest user is the USAF, which now has not only the 388th but also the 56th TFW at MacDill, the 474th at Nellis and the 363rd at Shaw, as well as the famed 8th (Wolf Pack) at Kunsan AB, South Korea. In 1982 deliveries even began to Air National Guard units. In addition the 50th TFW, at Hahn AB, Germany, brought F-16 muscle to the 4th ATAF from early 1982. Belgium's FAB flies F-16s with Nos 349 and 350 Sqns at Beauvechain and Nos 23 and 31 at Kleine Brogel, and in 1982 decided in principle to increase its buy from 116 to 160 to replace the Mirage 5BA. Denmark has so far bought 58, to equip Esk 727 and 730, 12 being two-seaters. The Netherlands bought an initial 102 but has already added the first of a planned annual increment of 22 additional F-16s, the first units to convert being 322/323 Sqns at Leeuwarden and then 311/312 at Volkel. In 1983-4 No 306 at Volkel, the dedicated photo-recon unit, was to switch to F-16s using the same installations and pods as the RF-104G. Norway bought an initial 72, painted non-standard uniform dark grey, and with an extended tail compartment for a braking parachute. First to convert was 332 Sqn at Rygge, followed by 331 at Bødo; 334 was fast converting in 1983 and instead of using Bullpup ASMs in the anti-ship role this unit will arm its F-16s with the indigenous Penguin 3.

Back in the U.S.A. a far-reaching MSIP (multinational staged improvement programme) has led to the future standard aircraft becoming the F-16C (single-seat) and D (two-seat). Larger tailplanes and Lantirn multisensor pods beside the inlets are the external features, but internally the differences are considerable, especially in the digital avionic architecture, the sensors and weapon-delivery systems for adverse conditions, and the cockpit displays and Marconi Avionics holographic HUD of unprecedented display size and qualities. General Dynamics has also flown prototypes of a larger tailless cranked-arrow F-16, the XL (F-16E) which can outmanoeuvre today's F-16 and carry twice the fuel or bomb load!

Above: Early F-16As from the 388th TFW, USAF, the original recipient, heading out for a practice bombing mission with two sizes of free-fall weapon. Accuracies are phenomenal.

Below: One of the first Dutch single-seaters, carrying only AIM-9J Sidewinder missiles. Though the F-16A on p.85 had a 306 Sqn badge, 322 was the first squadron to be equipped.

General Dynamics F-111

F-111A, D, E and F, FB-111A and EF-111A

Origin: (except EF) General Dynamics Corporation, (EF) Grumman Aerospace Corporation, both USA.

Type: A,D,E,F, all-weather attack; FB, strategic attack, EF, tactical ECM jammer.

Engines: Two Pratt & Whitney TF30 afterburning turbofans, as follows, (A,EF) 18,500lb (8,390kg) TF30-3, (D,E) 19,600lb (8,891kg) TF30-9, (FB) 20,350lb (9,231kg) TF30-7, (F) 25,100lb (11,385kg) TF30-100.

Dimensions: Span (fully spread) (A,D,E,F,EF) 63ft 0in (19.2m), (FB) 70ft 0in (21.34m), (fully swept) (A,D,E,F,EF) 31ft 11½in (9.74m) (FB) 33ft 11in (10.34m); length (except EF) 73ft 6in (22.4m), (EF) 77ft 1.6in (23.51m), wing area (A,D,E,F,EF, gross, 16°) 525sq ft (48.77m²).

Weights: Empty (A) 46,172lb (20,943kg), (D) 49,090lb (22,267kg) (E) about 47,000lb (21,319kg), (EF) 53,418lb (24,230kg), (F) 47,481lb (21,537kg), (FB) close to 50,000lb (22,680kg); loaded (A) 91,500lb (41,500kg), (D.E) 92,500lb (41,954kg), (F) 100,000lb (45,360kg), (FB) 114,300lb (51,846kg), (EF) 87,478lb (39,680kg).

Performance: Maximum speed at 36,000ft (11km), clean and with max afterburner, (A,D,E) Mach 2.2, 1,450mph (2,335km/h), (FB) Mach 2, 1,320mph (2,124km/h), (F) Mach 2.5, 1,653mph (2,660km/h), (EF) Mach 1.75; 1,160mph (1,865km/h); cruising speed, penetration, 571mph (919km/h); initial climb (EF) 3,592ft (1,950m)/min; service ceiling at combat weight, max afterburner, (A) 51,000ft (15,500m), (F) 60,000ft (18,290m), (EF) 54,700ft (16,670m); range with max internal fuel (A,D) 3,165 miles (5,093km), (F) 2,925 miles (4,707km), (EF) 2,484 miles (3,998km); takeoff run (A) 4,000ft (1,219m), (F) under 3,000ft (914m), (FB) 4,700ft (1,433m), (EF) 3,250ft (991m).

Armament: Internal weapon bay for two B43 bombs or (D,F) one B43 and one M61 gun; three pylons under each wing (four inboard swivelling with wing, outers being fixed and usable only at 16°, otherwise being jettisoned) for max external load 31,500lb (14,288kg), (FB only) provision for up to six SRAM, two internal, (EF) no armament.

History: First flight 21 December 1964; service delivery (A) June 1967, (EF) July 1981.

User: USA (Air Force).

Deployment: Though it was the centre of the biggest political row ever centred on any aircraft (partly because of failure to achieve a common design with the Navy, partly because many thought the wrong submission had been selected by the SecDef and his civilian aides against the advice of the uniformed Air Force, and partly because of extraordinarily severe technical problems and supposed shortcomings in nearly all the production aircraft), the F-111 was the first blind first-pass precision attack aircraft in the world, able to fly by night or in the worst weather direct to a small target, if necessary hugging the ground the whole way to avoid radar detection, ▶

Below: All F-111 attack aircraft are similar externally, but their capability varies considerably because of the different avionics and engine installations. This aircraft is an F-111A.

Above: Most 'Aardvarks' use only the four inboard pylons, and the basic design is such that the body cannot be used except for an ECM pod. Here 1,000lb bombs leave an F-111D.

Above: The Electric Fox (EF-111A) is an F-111A rebuilt by Grumman for electronic warfare.

▶and then drop a bomb on it. The basic F-111A version repeatedly demonstrated this capability in Vietnam, making brilliant and very courageous blind low-level attacks, using the terrain-following radar coupled to the flight control system, achieving complete surprise over the world's most heavily defended target, Hanoi/Haiphong. The F-111A still equips the 366th TFW at Mountain Home AFB, Idaho, and another US-based TFW is the 27th at Cannon AFB, New Mexico, which flies the F-111D, with extremely costly and quite different avionic systems. The FB-111A was developed for Strategic Air Command, and the 76 delivered equip two 30-aircraft wings, the 380th BW at Plattsburgh AFB and the 509th at Pease. These carry SRAM missiles or nuclear bombs, but in theory have the capability to drop a 41,250lb (18,711kg) load comprising 50 bombs of 825lb (nominal 750lb size). Most important to NATO are two wings based in southern England. The 20th TFW at Upper Heyford flies the F-111E and the 48th at Lakenheath flies the F-111F, with greatly uprated engines and improved avionics. Until the Tornado arrived these were the only all-weather precision attack aircraft in Europe, and even today nothing can equal their long range with typical attack loads. The unarmed EF-111A is a total rebuild by Grumman of a planned 42 F-111As to serve as sophisticated EW platforms.

Below: Badge of the 27th TFW (and TAC badge on the fin) shows this gun-equipped aircraft to be an F-111D (see photo on p.89).

Above: Probably taken from a tanker, this photograph shows an
F-111 (possibly an F-111A from Nellis) without pylons or tail code.

Grumman A-6 Intruder
Grumman A-6E, EA-6A and B, and KA-6D

Origin: Grumman Aerospace, USA.

Type: (A-6A, B, C, E) two-seat carrier-based all-weather attack; (EA-6A) two-seat ECM/attack; (EA-6B) four-seat ECM; (KA-6D) two-seat air-refuelling tanker.

Engines: (Except EA-6B) two 9,300lb (4,218kg) thrust Pratt & Whitney J52-8A turbojets; (EA-6B) two 11,200lb (5,080kg) J52-408.

Dimensions: Span 53ft (16.15m); length (except EA-6B) 54ft 7in (16.64m); (EA-6B) 59ft 5in (18.11m); height (A-6A, A-6C, KA-6D) 15ft 7in (4.75m); (A-6E, EA-6A and B) 16ft 3in (4.95m); wing area 528.9sq ft (49.1m^2).

Weights: Empty (A-6A) 25,684lb (11,650kg); (EA-6A) 27,769lb (12,596kg); (EA-6B) 34,581lb (15,686kg); (A-6E) 25,630lb (11,625kg); maximum loaded (A-6A and E) 60,400lb (27,397kg); (EA-6B) 58,500lb (26,535kg).

Performance: Maximum speed (clean A-6A) 685mph (1,102km/h) at sea level or 625mph (1,006km/h, Mach 0.94) at height; (EA-6A) over 630mph; (EA-6B) 599mph at sea level; (A-6E) 648mph (1,043km/h) at sea level; initial climb (A-6E, clean) 8,600ft (2,621m)/min; service ceiling (A-6A) 41,660ft (12,700m); (A-6E) 44,600ft (13,595m); (EA-6B) 39,000ft (11,582m); range with full combat load (A-6E) 1,077 miles (1,733km); ferry range with external fuel (all) about 3,100 miles (4,890km).

Armament: All attack versions, including EA-6A, five stores locations each rated at 3,600lb (1,633kg) with maximum total load of 15,000lb (6,804kg); typical load thirty 500lb (227kg) bombs; (EA-6B, KA-6D) none. ▶

Above: Despite its very high cost the EA-6B is proving a capable and often essential aircraft in any tactical situation. This example from CVW-17 (here operating from NAS Lemoore) is loaded with two tanks and three self-powered pods each housing two jamming transmitters.

Above: Taken during the Vietnam war this photograph shows an A-6A of VA-35 operating from USS *Enterprise*. Most Navy attack squadrons have since re-equipped with the updated A-6E.

History: First flight (YA2F-1) 19 April 1960; service acceptance of A-6A 1 February 1963; first flight (EA-6A) 1963; (KA-6D) 23 May 1966; (EA-6B) 25 May 1968; (A-6E) 27 February 1970; final delivery probably 1986.
User: USA (Navy, Marine Corps).

Deployment: With 13 giant carriers now in commission, the US Navy continues to build about 12 A-6E Intruder all-weather attack aircraft each year, both in order to form new squadrons and make good attrition (which is extremely low). By late 1982 a total of 15 squadrons had been activated in the Navy with the A-6E, each also having four KA-6D tankers. One or ▶

Below: Profile of an EA-6B Prowler, the standard electronic-warfare platform of the Air Wings. Each pod in the ALQ-99 system has its own windmill generator.

▶ two are always ashore, at Oceana for the Atlantic Fleet and Whidbey Island for the Pacific, and the rest are at sea embarked in one of the monster CVs or CVNs. In the European theatre the US Sixth Fleet is the dominant naval presence, and this has as its nucleus one or (usually) two carriers forming Carrier Group Two, Naples, the most likely ships being USS *Independence, JFK, Forrestal, Saratoga, America, Nimitz* or, possibly, the new *Carl Vinson.* The Vietnam war abundantly demonstrated the ability of the A-6 (usually in versions earlier than the E) to navigate and deliver accurately in bad weather or at night, and with the support of tankers and the EA-6B four-seat multi-waveband jammer aircraft the Navy's A-6 squadrons represent formidable striking power. The Marines do not normally operate in Europe but any long-term crisis would certainly see some of their five A-6E all-weather VMA(AW) attack squadrons committed to NATO's defence. Three Marine electronic warfare squadrons operate 15 EA-6Bs.

Right: These A-6A Intruders have now been converted into KA-6D tankers, and VA-176, though retaining the same tail code as part of CVW-6, flies from USS *America*. In this early version the avionics were voluminous and extensive but crew workload was high.

Below: Experience with this A-6A, an early version of Intruder, was of great value in planning today's A-6E, whose avionics are a generation later and an order of magnitude better. Probes are compatible with RAF tankers.

Above: Developed in 1950-56, the AGM-12 Bullpup was the first ASM (air-to-surface missile) to go into service after World War II.

Grumman F-14 Tomcat

F-14A and C

Origin: Grumman Aerospace, USA.

Type: Two-seat carrier-based multi-role fighter.

Engines: (F-14A) two 20,900lb (9,480kg) thrust Pratt & Whitney TF30-412A afterburning turbofans; (C) two 20,900lb (9,480kg) thrust Pratt & Whitney TF30-414A afterburning turbofans.

Dimensions: Span (68° sweep) 38ft 2in (11.63m), (20° sweep) 64ft 1½in (19.54m); length 62ft 8in (19.1m); height 16ft (4.88m); wing area (spread) 565sq ft (52.49m²).

Weights: Empty 37,500lb (17,010kg); loaded (fighter mission) 55,000lb (24,948kg), (maximum) 72,000lb (32,658kg).

Performance: Maximum speed, 1,564mph (2,517km/h, Mach 2.34) at height, 910mph (1,470km/h, Mach 1.2) at sea level; initial climb at normal gross weight, over 30,000ft (9,144m)/min; service ceiling over 56,000ft (17,070m); range (fighter with external fuel) about 2,000 miles (3,200km).

Armament: One 20mm M61A-1 multi-barrel cannon in fuselage; four AIM-7 Sparrow and four or eight AIM-9 Sidewinder air-to-air missiles, or up to six AIM-54 Phoenix and two AIM-9; maximum external weapon load in surface attack role 14,500lb (6,577kg).

History: First flight 21 December 1970; initial deployment with US Navy carriers October 1972; (F-14C) 1983.

User: USA (Navy).

Deployment: Developed to replace the unsuccessful F-111B, the F-14A was the best all-round fighting aircraft in the world in the early 1970s. Curiously, while the fixed-geometry F-15 is pressed into use as a low-level bomber (Strike Eagle), the variable-sweep F-14, which is ideally suited to all combat missions because of its swing-wings, has never operated in the

Below: 'Burners glow brightly as an F-14A in low-visibility camouflage is catapulted from a Navy carrier during NATO exercises off Norway in 1982. Also in the picture are two aircraft about to be shot from the adjacent bow catapult, an A-7E and S-3A. F-14 engine reliability has recently improved.

air/surface role though its potential is very considerable. By 1983 some 450 F-14s had been delivered, all of them (except for a handful on trials programmes) being assigned to one of 19 Navy fighter squadrons (VF), replacing the F-4 and in partnership with the E-2C Hawkeye control aircraft providing a quantum jump in capability. A single E-2C can direct 30 fighters simultaneously, and each F-14A can engage six individually selected targets at once over distances exceeding 100 miles (161km). The three basic missions of the F-14 are all forms of CAP (combat air patrol): Forcap is interceptor cover for the task force or friendly fleet; Barcap is barrier air defence against a major oncoming attack; and Tarcap is target cover for friendly attack aircraft in hostile airspace. No other aircraft has four stages of air/air weapons: guns, close-range Sidewinders, medium-range Sparrows ▶

Above: Carrying tanks, this unusually painted F-14A is loaded with four Phoenix, two Sparrows and two Sidewinders.

Below: F-14As of VF-32, fighter squadron embarked on *JFK* (which lost a Tomcat overboard off Scotland in 1976 but retrieved it).

▶ (later Amraam) and long-range Phoenix. Recent add-ons include the Northrop TCS (TV camera set) to provide greatly magnified images of distant targets, permitting visual identification, and the Tarps (tac air recon pod system) which fits in the belly tunnel and contains optical cameras and IR linescan. For many years dedicated RF-14 configurations have been studied as RA-5C replacements, but none has been ordered and Tarps is a temporary way of filling the gap, with 48 F-14s thus equipped. Budget limitations prevented implementation of the 1970 plan for successive improved F-14s but the more serious deficiencies of the F-14A, in engine reliability and avionics, are rectified in the F-14C which replaced the F-14A in production in 1983. No decision has been taken on the much better and more powerful GE F101-DFE engine flown in the 'Super Tomcat' in 1981.

Above: Launch of an AIM-54 Phoenix missile is not an everyday event, mainly because of extremely high cost. This F-14A serves with VF-24 'Checkertails' from USS *Constellation*.

Right: Another F-14A from VF-32 loaded in this case with the maximum of six AIM-54A Phoenix long-range missiles.

Below: Today virtually all the Tomcats in embarked Air Wings are painted in low-contrast grey. This example, from VF-33 is just landing aboard *Independence*.

Lockheed F-104 Starfighter

F-104G, S, CF-104, QF-104, RF and RTF-104, TF-104 (data for F-104G)

Origin: Lockheed-California Co, USA; (CF) Canadair; (S) Aeritalia.

Type: (G) multimission strike fighter; (CF) strike-reconnaissance; (TF) dual trainer; (QF) drone RPV; (F-104S) all-weather interceptor; (RF and RTF) reconnaissance.

Engine: One General Electric J79 turbojet with afterburner; (G, RF/RTF, CF) 15,800lb (7,167kg) J79-11A; (S) 17,900lb (8,120kg) J79-19 or J1Q.

Dimensions: Span (without tip tanks) 21ft 11in (6.68m); length 54ft 9in (16.69m); height 13ft 6in (4.11m); wing area 196.1sq ft (18.22m²).

Weights: Empty 14,082lb (6,387kg), (F-104S, 14,900lb, 6,760kg); maximum loaded 28,779lb (13,054kg), (F-104S, 31,000lb, 14,060kg).

Performance: Maximum speed 1,450mph (2,334km/h, Mach 2.2); initial climb 50,000ft (15,250m)/min; service ceiling 58,000ft (17,680m) (zoom ceiling over 90,000ft, 27,400m); range with maximum weapons, about 300 miles (483km); range with four drop tanks (high altitude, subsonic) 1,815 miles (2,920km).

Armament: In most versions, centreline rack rated at 2,000lb (907kg) and two underwing pylons each rated at 1,000lb (454kg); additional racks for small missiles (eg Sidewinder) on fuselage, under wings or on tips; certain versions have reduced fuel and one 20mm M61 Vulcan multi-barrel gun in fuselage; (S) M61 gun, two Sparrow or Aspide and two Sidewinder.

History: First flight (XF-104) 7 February 1954; (F-104A) 17 February 1956; (F-104G) 5 October 1960; (F-104S) 30 December 1968; final delivery from United States 1964; final delivery from Aeritalia (F-104S) 1975.

Users: Belgium, Canada, Denmark, W Germany, Greece, Italy, Netherlands, Norway, Spain, Turkey, USA (ANG).

Deployment: Clarence L. ("Kelly") Johnson planned the Model 83 after talking with fighter pilots in Korea in 1951. The apparent need was for ▶

Above: With the rather rapid withdrawal of F-104Gs the F-104S is now probably the most important NATO Starfighter variant. The chief user is Italy's AMI, which however still has 28 TF-104G trainers in the 20° Gruppo based at Grosseto.

Left: Greece still uses a few single-and two-seat F-104s as advanced trainers at Araxos, including this Canadair 104G.

Below: More powerful and updated in many other ways, the Aeritalia F-104S has proved a cost/effective investment able to fly interception and low-level attack missions. Aircraft from AMI 4° Stormo.

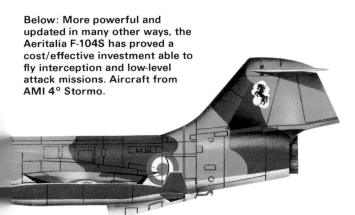

▶ superior flight performance, even at the expense of reduced equipment and weapons or fuel. The original models carried only an M61 gun and two Sidewinders, but in 1960 the Luftwaffe picked the specially designed F-104G as its chief tactical warplane, with tremendous low-level penetrative capability with radar mapping and a nuclear bomb. Other NATO partners followed suit and 1,266 F-104Gs were built in a vast multinational programme centred on Federal Germany, Benelux countries and Italy, plus 200 CF-104s and 181 two-seat TF-104Gs. From 1965 until 1980 these were the most numerous, and to European NATO air forces, the most important of all types of combat aircraft. Today, however, the Luftwaffe and Marineflieger are steadily replacing various single- and two-seat variants with the far more capable Tornado, while Belgium, the Netherlands, Denmark and Norway are replacing F-104s with the dramatically superior F-16. Nevertheless, large numbers of slightly worn Starfighters continue to do a fine job, not only with the nations listed but also with Greece and Turkey, while in Italy much newer aircraft serve in the interceptor role.

   Though the F-104G got a bad name for its apparently high accident record with the Luftwaffe, this was the result of inexperienced flight and ground staff and the use of nearly 1,000 aircraft, and certainly did not reflect a defective weapon system. At the same time the basic aircraft is totally unforgiving, demands a good runway surface (though the length is seldom critical, ground runs rarely exceeding 3,000ft/900m) and almost any major inflight emergency results in ejection. The low attack or recon mission is flown well, the aircraft presenting a very small and usually smokeless target which in the clean condition and with high fuel consumption can work up to 790kt (910mph, 1,464km/h). Most, however, have no internal EW system, and standard Gs have only three pylons (apart from wingtip Sidewinders) so ECM pods sterilize one-third of the payload. ▶

Above: Here seen in service with the AMI's 23° Gruppo, 5° Stormo, Rimini-Miramare, the F-104S has the Autonetics R21G radar optimised for air combat and capable of guiding Sparrow and Aspide.

Left: In contrast the Canadian Armed Forces have ignored the air-to-air mission and both equip their CF-104s and plan their training on ground attack mission. This aircraft is rocketing at Cold Lake training base.

Below: Once by far the most numerous front-line combat aircraft in Western Europe, the F-104G (and sub-variants) of the Luftwaffe are being replaced by Tornados as are the Marineflieger's whose MFG 2 is now almost converted. Most have gone to other NATO nations.

► Such has been the pace of F-16 deliveries that few F-104s will remain in Belgium, Denmark, the Netherlands or Norway by the time this book appears, and though in 1981 the Luftwaffe still had 330 plus 32 two-seaters, half these will have been withdrawn by late 1983. The Marineflieger's MFG 1 will probably be an all-Tornado unit when this book appears, and the big Luftwaffe training force at Luke AFB is winding down. Canada, however, must keep its CF-104s until 1985-6, during which period the CF-18 will take over. The CAF 1st CAG at Baden-Soellingen deploys about 70 CF-104s and a few two-seat CF-104Ds in the conventional attack and recon roles, with back-up training aircraft at Cold Lake, Alberta. Greece's 335 and 336 squadrons at Araxos will fly F-104Gs and TFs for at least the next five years even if a newer aircraft were to be ordered in 1983. Turkey's 141 and 191 squadrons likewise fly secondhand machines in the

attack role, with small prospect of a replacement until after 1986. Turkey also has two squadrons (142 and 181) flying the F-104S interceptor, bought new from Aeritalia (40 aircraft). The S was a joint US/Italian creation with air/air avionics and weapons, a more powerful engine and various other improvements. In Italy the AMI bought 205 of this type, plus 30 RF-104G recon platforms and 20 TF trainers. Over 40 have been written off, but the S has proved an effective interceptor used under Nadge control, with a gun, Sidewinders and medium-range Sparrow or Aspide AAMs. It equips three gruppi in this role, and a further seven in the strike role

Below: A beautiful picture of F-104S interceptors of the AMI's 5° Stormo 'Giuseppi Cenni' based at Rimini-Miramare. They are carrying maximum fuel but no missiles, an unusual combination.

McDonnell Douglas A-4 Skyhawk

A-4A to A-4Y, OA-4M and TA-4 series

Origin: Douglas Aircraft (division of McDonnell Douglas), USA.

Type: Single-seat attack bomber; OA, two-seat FAC; TA, dual-control trainer.

Engine: (E, J) 8,500lb (3,856kg) Pratt & Whitney J52-6 turbojet; (F, G, H, K) 9,300lb (4,218kg) J52-8A; (M, N, Y) 11,200lb (5,080kg) J52-408A.

Dimensions: Span 27ft 6in (8.38m); length (E, F, G, H, K, L, P, Q, S) 40ft 1½in (12.22m), (M,N,Y,) 40ft 3¼in (12.27m), (OA, and TA, excluding probe) 42ft 7¼in (12.98m); height 15ft (4.57m), (TA series 15ft 3in).

Weights: Empty (E) 9,284lb, (typical single-seat, eg Y) 10,465lb (4,747kg), (TA-4F) 10,602 (4,809kg); maximum loaded (shipboard) 24,500lb (11,113kg); (land-based) 27,420lb (12,437kg).

Performance: Maximum speed (clean) (E) 685mph, (Y) 670mph (1,078km/h), (TA-4F) 675mph; maximum speed (4,000lb 1,814kg bomb load) (Y) 645mph; initial climb (Y) 8,440ft (2,572m)/min; service ceiling (all, clean) about 49,000ft (14,935m); range (clean, or with 4,000lb weapons and max fuel, all late versions) about 920 miles (1,480km); maximum range (Y) 2,055 miles (3,307km).

Armament: Standard on most versions, two 20mm Mk 12 cannon, each with 200 rounds; (H, N, and optional on other export versions) two 30mm DEFA 553, each with 150 rounds. Pylons under fuselage and wings for total ordnance load of (E, F, G, H, K, L, P, Q, S) 8,200lb (3,720kg); (M, N, Y) 9,155lb (4,153kg).

History: First flight (XA4D-1) 22 June 1954; (A-4A) 14 August 1954; squadron delivery October 1956; (A-4M) April 1970; (A-4N) June 1972; first of TA series (TA-4E) June 1965, (OA) 1979.

User: USA (Marine Corps).

Deployment: One of the world's most cost/effective attack aircraft, the compact, hard-hitting and beautifully engineered Skyhawk was in continuous production for 26 years (1954-79). It has been acquired new and secondhand by air forces and navies all over the world, and in Vietnam was used by the US Navy, Marine Corps and Air Force, but it never found its way to any NATO nation outside the USA. Even here it is now used operationally only by the Marines, where it serves in several new-build or remanufactured single-seat attack versions, as well as the OA-4M FAC (forward air control) model. The chief operational model is the A-4Y, some of which were the final new-build aircraft while others are rebuilt A-4Ms with the Marconi Avionics HUD, an advanced ARBS (angle/rate bombing system) and other updates including enhanced EW systems. The OA-4M is a rebuild of the

Right: Air-to-air missiles are not normally carried, but this 'Camel' rebuilt A-4C (150586), then with VA-55, is launching an AGM-45 Shrike anti-radar missile, derived from the AIM-7 Sparrow. Tail code NP is no longer used.

Above: The Skyhawk's tall but narrow landing gear was expected to cause deck stability problems, but did not in use.

Below: Built as an A4D-2N, this Skyhawk became an A-4C in 1962. It served with VA-83 (later re-equipped with A-7E).

TA-4F trainer, 23 having been completely remanufactured by the Naval Air Rework Facility at Pensacola. Any of these could suddenly become involved in NATO affairs, but in peacetime are unlikely to be seen in Europe. Most USMC A-4s will be replaced by the AV-8B from 1985.

McDonnell Douglas/BAe AV-8 Harrier

AV-8A, TAV-8A, AV-8C, VA-1, VAE-1

Origin: British Aerospace, UK; marketed and supported by McDonnell Aircraft (MCAIR), USA.

Type: STOVL light attack (land or ship based).

Engine: One 21,500lb (9,752kg) thrust RR Pegasus 103 (Pratt & Whitney F402-402) vectored-thrust turbofan.

Dimensions: Span 25ft 3in (7.7m); length 45ft 8in (13.92m), (two-seat) 55ft 9½in (17.0m); height 11ft 4in (3.43m), (two-seat) 13ft 8in (4.17m); wing area 201.1sq ft (18.68m²).

Weights: Empty 12,300lb (5,579kg), (two-seat, with ballast) 13,300lb (6,033kg); maximum 25,000lb (11,340kg).

Performance: Maximum speed (clean, SL) 740mph (1,191km/h); dive limit Mach 1.3; radius (32.2°C day, 3,000lb/1,361kg ordnance, lo profile) 58 miles (93km) from VTO, 437 miles (703km) from 1,200ft/366m run.

Armament: All external, provision for two 30mm Aden guns with 150 rounds each; two Sidewinder AAMs pylons, plus normal weapon load of 3,000lb (1,361kg) on centreline and inboard pylons (max weapon load, including guns, 5,000lb, 2,268kg).

History: Prototypes as Harrier; delivery of first AV-8A 20 November 1970, (VA-1) 1976, (AV-8C) 1979.

Users: Spain (Navy), USA (Marine Corps).

Deployment: The US Marine Corps found in the original Harrier a totally new kind of weapon, which could operate from anywhere a helicopter could go yet provide the performance and firepower of a jet fighter. Very much against the opposition of the Congressional/aerospace lobby, and contrary to the professed belief of the Air Force, the corps boldly purchased 102 AV-8A Harriers differing from the GR.3 mainly in having a simpler avionic fit, with the inertial nav/attack system removed, and with a modified weapon-aiming Hudwac (head-up display, weapon-aiming computer) and Sidewinders on outer-wing pylons. In 1979-84 the 61 surviving AV-8As were being remanufactured at MCAS Cherry Point, with support by BAe and MCAIR, to emerge as AV-8Cs with lift-improvement devices, enhanced avionics and new EW installations. The USMC also bought eight two-seat TAV-8As, similar to the RAF's T.4. The Spanish Navy bought 11 VA-1 Matadors, similar to the AV-8A but with additional voice radio, for use by Escuadron 008 from the carrier *Dedalo* (to be replaced by the new *Principe de Asturias* in 1985-6), with Rota as land base, plus two VAE-1 two-seaters. The AV-8s and VA-1s have operated intensively, mainly in the close-support role from both land airstrips and various types of ship, and all are due to be replaced by AV-8Bs late in the decade.

Below: Spain's Arma Aérea de la Armada operates the Harrier as the VA-1 (two-seater is VAE-1) in Esc 008 with home base at Rota. The AV-8B is to follow later in the decade.

Above: Two US Marine Corps AV-8A Harriers operating from an unprepared site in the mid-1970s. This experience was of value in planning the AV-8C update and all-new AV-8B Harrier II.

McDonnell Douglas/BAe AV-8B Harrier II

AV-8B, Harrier GR.5

Origin: McDonnell Aircraft (MCAIR, St Louis), with British Aerospace as principal subcontractor.

Type: STOVL multi-role attack (probably also reconnaissance).

Engine: One 21,500lb (9,752kg) thrust Pratt & Whitney F402-404 (RR Pegasus 11-21E) vectored-thrust turbofan.

Dimensions: Span 30ft 4in (9.25m); length 46ft 4in (14.12m); height 11ft 8in (3.56m); wing area 230sq ft (21.37m²).

Weights: Empty 12,750lb (5,783kg); maximum (VTO) 19,185lb (8,702kg), (STO) 29,750lb (1,349kg).

Performance: Maximum Mach number in level flight 0.91 (at sea level, 692mph, 1,113km/h); combat radius (STO, seven Mk 82 bombs plus tanks, lo profile, no loiter) 748 miles (1,204km); ferry range 2,879 miles (4,633km).

Armament: Seven external pylons, centreline rated at 1,000lb (454kg) inboard wing 2,000lb (907kg), centre wing 1,000lb (454kg) and outboard 630lb (286kg), for total external load of 7,000lb (3,175kg) for VTO or 17,000lb (7,711kg) for STO; in addition ventral gun pods for (US) one 25mm GAU-12/U gun and ammunition or (RAF) two 30mm Aden.

History: First flight (YAV-8B rebuild) 9 November 1978, (AV-8B) November 1981; entry into service (AV-8B) 1983, (GR.5) 1986.

Users: (AV-8B) USA (Marine Corps, possibly also Navy); later Spain (Navy), (GR.5) UK (RAF).

Below: This view shows the new graphite-composite wing of the AV-8B Harrier II, though not LERX root extension. Largest single increment in extra VTO lift was gained by improved circulation round the inner wing with large-chord flaps depressed.

Above: Still one of the smallest modern combat aircraft, the AV-8B has by careful detail improvement been made either to carry double the bombload of original Harrier or fly twice the distance.

Development: Foolishly the UK Defence Minister, Roy Mason, said in March 1975 that there was "not enough common ground" for the RAF and US Marine Corps requirements for a second-generation Harrier to go ahead as a joint project. The inevitable result was that, after more than two years of timewasting, the AV-8B was accepted by the RAF in July 1981 (in preference to BAe's purpose-designed Harrier GR.5) and a collaborative deal was agreed between McDonnell Douglas and BAe. Under its terms the US Marine Corps will receive four FSD (full-scale development) aircraft plus 336 production AV-8B Harrier IIs, while the RAF will receive 60 Harrier GR.5s, structurally identical but with different avionics and guns, assembled at Kingston/Dunsfold. The work is split 60 per cent to MCAIR and 40 to BAe, but export sales to third countries are split 75/25, the first of these being Spain which will receive 12 AV-8Bs at a cost of $379 million. Compared with the first-generation Harrier the Harrier II has a completely re-engineered airframe, with a new graphite-composite wing of much greater span, large flaps, improved engine nozzles and inlets, and many ▶

▶ other changes which provide 50 per cent more internal fuel and a much greater weapon load, the mission radius or weapon load being approximately doubled with virtually no increase in engine thrust (there is a very small gain in thrust, but the Dash-404 engine is aimed chiefly at extending life and reliability and reducing cost). In 1981 the full-scale development programme began with a fatigue and a static test airframe at St Louis, followed by four flight FSD aircraft, all of which are camouflaged and have improved lift-augmentation devices and added semicircular LERX (leading-edge root extensions) developed by BAe. The US aircraft have the gun in one ventral pod and the ammunition in the other while the gun pods of the RAF GR.5 are the same as in previous Harriers. Avionics include an

Above: On test near St Louis, the Harrier II is here fitted with the definitive wing with LERX. In January 1983 one of the pre-production machines made the first 'hands off' automatic vertical landing controlled by its new digital autopilot. Advanced cockpit and repositioned reaction-control valves reduce workload.

advanced cockpit display and Smiths HUD, ring-laser gyro, ARBS (angle rate bombing system) and comprehensive passive warning system, chaff/flare dispenser and centreline ECM pod (ALQ-164). In the US Marine Corps the Harrier II will replace remaining A-4 Skyhawks followed by AV-8Cs, while in the RAF the GR.5 will replace existing Harriers. The AV-8B is configured very much as a bomber, with considerably enhanced weapon load and range compared with existing Harriers, and improved avionics. The RAF wanted improved air-combat capability and though the GR.5 will have better turn radius this still falls short of requirements, as does maximum speed. Work continues on developing a supersonic STOVL combat aircraft with a PCB (plenum-chamber burning) engine.

Below: Though it looks similar the raised canopy of the Harrier II is not the same as that of the Sea Harrier, though it gives an equally good all-round view.

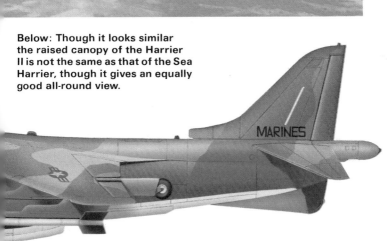

McDonnell Douglas F-4 Phantom II

F-4C to S and RF-4

Origin: McDonnell Aircraft, division of McDonnell Douglas, USA.

Type: Originally carrier-based all-weather interceptor; now all-weather multi-role fighter for ship or land operation; (F-4G) EW defence suppression; (RF) all-weather multisensor reconnaissance.

Engines: (C, D, RF) two 17,000lb (7,711kg) General Electric J79-15 turbojets with afterburner; (E, F, G) 17,900lb (8,120kg) J79-17; (J, N, S) 17,900lb J79-10; (K, M) 20,515lb (9,305kg) Rolls-Royce Spey 202/203 augmented turbofans.

Dimensions: Span 38ft 5in (11.7m); length (C, D, J, N, S) 58ft 3in (17.76m), (E, G, F and all RF versions) 62ft 11in or 63ft (19.2m), (K, M) 57ft 7in (17.55m); height (all) 16ft 3in (4.96m); wing area 530sq ft (49.2m²).

Weights: Empty (C, D, J, N) 28,000lb (12,700kg), (E, F and RF) 29,000lb (13,150kg), (G, K, M) 31,000lb (14,060kg); maximum loaded (C, D, J, K, M, N, RF) 58,000lb (26,308kg), (E, G, F) 60,630lb (27,502kg).

Performance: Maximum speed with Sparrow missiles only (low) 910mph (1,464km/h, Mach 1.19) with J79 engines, 920mph with Spey, (high) 1,500mph (2,414km/h, Mach 2.27) with J79, 1,386mph with Spey; initial climb, typically 28,000ft (8,534m)/min with J79, 32,000ft/min with Spey; service ceiling, over 60,000ft (19,685m) with J79, 60,000ft with Spey; range on internal fuel (no weapons) about 1,750 miles (2,817km); ferry range with external fuel, typically 2,300 miles (3,700km), (E and variants), 2,600 miles (4,184km).

Armament: (All versions except RF models which have no armament) four

Above: Spain's Ejercito del Aire uses the F-4CR(S) with the designation C-12. A total of 33 were supplied to equip Esc 121 and Esc 122 both based at Torrejón.

Right: Whereas USAF Phantoms have a boom receptacle those of the US Navy and Marine Corps use the retractable probe, compatible with US or British tankers.

Above: Flightline maintenance for an F-4D's Westinghouse radar.

AIM-7 Sparrow or Sky Flash (later Amraam) air-to-air missiles recessed under fuselage; inner wing pylons can carry two more AIM-7 or four AIM-9 Sidewinder missiles; in addition E versions except RF have internal 20mm M61 multi-barrel gun, and virtually all versions can carry the same gun in external centreline pod; all except RF have centreline and four wing pylons for tanks, bombs or other stores to total weight of 16,000lb (7,257kg).

History: First flight (XF4H-1) 27 May 1958; service delivery (F-4A) February 1961 (inventory); first flight (Air Force F-4C) 27 May 1963; (F-4E) 30 June 1967; (F-4G) 1976.

Users: W Germany, Greece, Spain, Turkey, UK (RAF), USA (Air Force, ANG, Navy, Marine Corps). ▶

▶ **Deployment:** Unquestionably the world's No 1 warplane of the 1960s and still one of the most important in the NATO nations, the F-4 was designed as a carrier-based naval fighter armed only with AAMs. It proved by superior performance its fitness for such roles as land-based interception, long-range attack, multisensor reconnaissance and service as an advanced EW (electronic warfare) defence-suppression aircraft. In its country of origin it has for many years slowly been withdrawn and replaced by the F-14 and F-15, and remaining US Navy F-4s (mostly of the F-4J and S varieties) are now progressively being replaced by the F/A-18A. In early 1983, however, the F-4 was still extremely important to USAFE, equipping the 52nd TFW at Spangdahlem (F-4E and G), 86th at Ramstein (E), 401st at Torrejón (C) and 406th TFT (various sub-types) at Zaragoza, while the RF-4C equips the 10th TRW at RAF Alconbury and the 26th TRW at Zweibrücken. The F-4G, so far operated only by the USAF, is a rebuild of late-model F-4E fighters with the APR-38 EW system whose 52 special aerials (antennae) include large pods facing forwards under the nose and to the rear above the rudder. The system is governed by a Texas Instruments computer with reprogrammable software to keep up to date on all known hostile emitters. This Phantom carries such weapons as triplets of the AGM-65 EO-guided Maverick precision attack weapon, Shrike ARM (anti-radar missile) and HARM (high-speed ARM). Like almost all Phantoms the left front fuselage recess often carries an ECM jammer pod (usually an ALQ-119), leaving the other three available for Sparrow AAMs if necessary; or Sidewinders can be carried under the wings. The F-4G makes a considerable difference to the effectiveness of a strike by friendly aircraft through defended territory, by sensing, locating and destroying many of the most dangerous ground defence systems. Although there is an obvious need for them, curiously no ▶

Top: Taken before the RAF standardized on the B-type roundel, this photo shows an echelon of a USAF F-4E, RAF FGR.2 and Luftwaffe RF-4E.

Above: A Westinghouse ALQ-119 (V) ECM pod is in the left front AAM recess of this F-4D-28 formerly used by the 81st TFS at Spangdahlem AB, Germany (today an F-4G operator).

Left: This RAF Phantom FGR.2 over Scarborough, Yorkshire, is burdened with seven BL. 755 cluster bombs, four Sparrows and two pairs of AIM-9B Sidewinders.

Right: A unique type operated by the Luftwaffe is the RF-4E, one of which is seen operating with AG 52 based at Leck. This F-4 variant fits the recon systems of the RF-4C into the uprated airframe of the F-4E. The photo was taken on 16 October 1970 when these F-4s were quite new. The West German Luftwaffe has two Aufklärungsgeschwader (recon wings), each with 30 of these aircraft.

▶ EW conversions have appeared in NATO air forces in Western Europe.

Federal Germany's Luftwaffe received 175 F-4F Phantoms, which since the mid-1970s have comprised virtually the whole of the key NATO nation's fighter force on the Central Sector. Originally these were simplified F-4Es, without many of the USAF avionics and used purely in the interception role, equipping JG 71 at Wittmundhafen and JG 74 at Neuburg. Equipped for surface attack the same number (80) equip JaboG 35 at Pferdsfeld and JaboG 36 at Rheine-Hopsten. The Luftwaffe also purchased 88 of a unique sub-type (which was later exported to other customers), the RF-4E, the unarmed multisensor conversion of the F-4E. About 40 equip AG 51 at Bremgarten and another 40 AG 52 at Leck. Since 1980 the Luftwaffe has been trying to get more out of its big Phantom force. The RF-4Es are progressively being reworked by MBB to emerge as dual-role recon or attack aircraft (though it is not possible to carry all recon sensors and also deliver bombs on the same mission). The F-4Fs are being upgraded to fire the US Amraam missile, when this is developed; this requires substantial changes to the radar and it is speculated that new radars will soon be fitted, the APG-65 (F/A-18A) being suggested. Greece has three 18-strong F-4E squadrons (337 at Larissa and 338 and 339 at Andravida) in the attack role. Spain has two 18-aircraft squadrons (121 and 122) of

F-4CR(S) based at Torrejón in the fighter role, plus four RF-4Cs. Turkey received 86 F-4Es, deployed among 113 Filo at Eskisehir (which also has eight RF-4Es), 162 at Bandirma, and 171/172 at Erhac-Malataya; all four squadrons are tasked mainly in the strike role.

The UK's Phantoms are unlike all other variants in having Spey turbofan engines, which give much more thrust at low level and reduced fuel burn in most flight regimes but whose installation caused severe problems and results in high drag which nullifies the extra thrust and even results in slightly poorer maximum speed and ceiling. A total of 52 F-4K were supplied to the RN as Phantom FG.1 and 118 F-4M to the RAF as the FGR.2. Today RAF Germany (2 ATAF) has two squadrons of FGR.2s (19 and 92) at Wildenrath, while in the UK the same type equips No 23 and 56 at Wattisham, 29 and 64 (the OCU) at Coningsby, and 111 and 43 at Leuchars, Scotland (43 has the FG.1, some of which are stored). All fly in the interception role with Sky Flash AAMs, and are still adequate though due to be replaced by the Tornado F.2 in the second half of the decade. All RAF Phantoms have ARI.18228 EW warning with the receiver aerials in fin-top fairings; ECM pods have been in short supply and obsolescent (mostly ALQ-101) but a better pod may one day be found (ARI.23246/1 is for Tornado only).

Left: A profile of a Luftwaffe RF-4E, again serving with AG 52 from Leck. Though nominal AG strength is 30, in fact each wing has about 40 aircraft with ten in store for attrition. They are being modified to carry out a limited range of attack missions.

McDonnell Douglas F-15 Eagle

F-15A,B,C,D and E

Origin: McDonnell Aircraft Company, USA.

Type: Air-superiority fighter with secondary attack role.

Engines: Two 23,930lb (10,855kg) thrust Pratt & Whitney F100-100 afterburning turbofans.

Dimensions: Span 42ft 9¾in (13.05m); length (all) 63ft 9in (19.43m), height 18ft 7½in (5.68m); wing area 608sq ft (56.5m²).

Weights: Empty (basic equipped) 28,000lb (12.7t); loaded (interception mission, max internal fuel plus four AIM-7, F-15A) 41,500lb (18,824kg), (C) 44,500lb (20,185kg); maximum with max external load (A) 56,500lb (25,628kg), (C) 68,000lb (30,845kg).

Performance: Maximum speed (over 36,000ft/10,973m with no external load except four AIM-7), 1,653mph (2,660km/h, Mach 2.5), with max external load or at low level, not published; initial climb (clean) over 50,000ft (15.24km)/min, (max wt) 29,000ft (8.8km)/min; service ceiling 65,000ft (19.8km); takeoff run (clean) 900ft (274m); landing run (clean, without brake chute) 2,500ft (762m); ferry range with three external tanks, over 2,878 miles (4,631km), (with Fast packs also) over 3,450 miles (5,560km).

Armament: One 20mm M61A-1 gun with 940 rounds, four AIM-7F (later Amraam) fitting against fuselage, four AIM-9L (later Asraam) on flanks of wing pylons, total additional ordnance load 16,000lb (7,257kg) on five stations (two each wing, one centreline).

History: First flight (A) 27 July 1972, (B) 7 July 1973, service delivery (Cat II test) March 1974, (inventory) November 1974.

User: USA (Air Force). ▶

Below: Three F-15As from the 36th TFW (Bitburg AB, West Germany) seen over Norway on exercise Arctic Express '78.

Above: Probably the same three aircraft are about to leave Bødo AB, Norway, where they were on detachment from Bitburg.

► **Deployment:** Recognizing its urgent need for a superior long-range air-combat fighter, the Air Force issued an RFP in September 1968 for the FX, the McDonnell proposal being selected in late 1969, with the F100 engine and Hughes APG-63 radar following in 1970. Inevitably the demand for long range resulted in a large aircraft, the wing having to be so large to meet the manoeuvre requirement that it has a fixed leading edge and plain unblown trailing-edge flaps. Two of the extremely powerful engines were needed to achieve the desired ratio of thrust/weight, which near sea level in the clean condition exceeds unity. The lower edge of the fuselage is tailored to snug fitting of four medium-range AAMs. The gun is in the bulged strake at the root of the right wing, drawing ammunition from a tank inboard of the duct. There is no fuel between the engines but abundant room in the integral-tank inner wing and between the ducts for 11,600lb (5,260kg, 1,448 gal, 6,592lit), and three 250 gal (2,270lit) drop tanks can be carried, each stressed to 5g manoeuvres when full. Roll is by ailerons only at low speeds, the dogtoothed slab tailplanes taking over entirely at over Mach 1, together with the twin rudders, which are vertical.

Avionics and flight/weapon control systems are typical of the 1970 period, with a flat-plate scanner pulse-doppler radar, vertical situation display presenting ADI (attitude/director indicator), radar and EO information on one picture, a HUD, INS and central digital computer. In its integral ECM/IFF subsystems the F-15 was far better than most Western fighters, with Loral radar warning (with front/rear aerials on the left fin tip), Northrop ALQ-135 internal counter-measures system, Magnavox EW warning set and Hazeltine APX-76 IFF with Litton reply-evaluator. High-power jammers, however, must still be hung externally, Westinghouse ►

Below: From the mid-1980s the medium-range missile carried by F-15s will be the new Amraam, one of which is here seen on an early compatibility firing test. Later the advanced Sidewinder models will also be replaced, probably by a European Asraam.

Above: An F-15C used for missile firing tests seen in clean condition apart from centreline tank and red instrumentation link.

Above: Eagles from the 33rd TFW, Eglin AFB, with Canadian CF-104 on Exercise Reforger '82.

Left: An early production F-15A in service with the 58th Tac Fighter Wing based at Luke AFB, Arizona. This wing is comprised of the 461st, 550th and 551st Tac Fighter Sqns, with weapons training performed at Nellis AFB by the 57th Tac Trg Wing.

▶ pods normally occupying an outer wing pylon. The APG-63 offered excellent capability to track low-level targets, with cockpit switches giving a Hotas (Hands on throttle and stick) capability which dramatically improved dogfight performance. Though it was, and remains, concerned at the price, the Air Force got in the F-15A everything it was looking for, and in many respects the F-15 has from its entry to service generally been regarded as the world's No 1 fighter (as was the F-4 before it).

USAF procurement is now extending beyond the original planned force level of 729, partly to replace the F-106 for US home defence and partly for fresh missions which by the time this book appears may include all-weather strike (F-15E, derived from the company-funded Strike Eagle). Current production is centred on the F-15C and two-seat F-15D. These provide substantial updates in mission capability. A programmable signal processor gives the ability to switch from one locked-on target to another, to switch between air and ground targets and keep searching whilst already locked-on to one or more targets. Increase in memory capacity from 24 to 96K gives a new high-resolution radar mode which can pick one target from a large group at extreme range. (This calls for Sky Flash, but the USAF will wait until Amraam has been developed.) Internal fuel is increased by 2,000lb (907kg) and conformal pallets, called Fast packs (Fuel And Sensor, Tactical) fit snugly on each side of the fuselage to increase total fuel by no less than 9,750lb (4,422kg).

Almost all the original 729 Eagles had been delivered by the time this book appeared. Recipient units began with the 57th TTW at Nellis, and followed with the 58th TTW at Luke, 1st TFW at Langley (the pre-eminent 'fire brigade' outfit, experienced in rapid overseas deployment), 49th TFW at Holloman, 33rd TFW at Eglin and 18th TFW at Okinawa, followed by former F-106 units starting with the 48th FIS. In USAFE the F-15 equips the 36th TFW at Bitburg and the 32nd TFS at Camp Amsterdam (Soesterberg, Netherlands). Existing USAFE F-4 units will convert to the F-15 in the course of 1983-5. Several NATO nations have eyed the F-15, but price and operating costs put it out of reach.

Above: Four single-seaters (probably F-15Cs) from 1st TFW, Langley AFB, Virginia, part of the Rapid Deployment Force.

Below: Wide-angle photo taken by the backseater in F-15B of 49th TFW from Holloman showing hook-up to a KC-10A Extender.

McDonnell Douglas/Northrop F/A-18 Hornet

F/A-18A, TF/A-18A, CF-18.

Origin: McDonnell Douglas Corp, USA, with Northrop building centre and aft fuselage.

Type: (F/A) single-seat carrier-based multi-role fighter, (TF) dual trainer, (CF) single-seat land-based attack fighter.

Engines: Two 16,000lb (7,257kg) thrust General Electric F404-400 augmented turbofans.

Dimensions: Span (with missiles) 40ft 4¾in (12.31m), (without missiles) 37ft 6in (11.42m); length 56ft (17.07m); height 15ft 3½in (4.66m); wing area 400sq ft (37.16m²).

Weights: (Provisional) empty 20,583lb (9,336kg); loaded (clean) 33,642lb (15,260kg); loaded (attack mission) 47,000lb (21,319kg); maximum loaded (catapult limit) 50,064lb (22,710kg).

Performance: Maximum speed (clean, at altitude) 1,190mph (1,915km/h, Mach 1.8), (maximum weight, sea level) subsonic; sustained combat manoeuvre ceiling, over 49,000ft (14,935m); combat radius (air-to-air mission, high, no external fuel) 461 miles (741km); ferry range, more than 2,300 miles (3,700km).

Armament: One 20mm M61 Gatling in upper part of forward fuselage; nine external weapon stations for maximum load (catapult launch) of 13,400lb (6,080kg) or (land takeoff) of 17,000lb (7,711kg), including bombs, sensor pods, (ECM missiles (including Sparrow) and other stores, with tip-mounted Sidewinders.

History: First flight (YF-17) 9 June 1974; (first of 11 test F-18) 18 November 1978; (production F/A-18) 1980; service entry, 1982.

Users: Canada, Spain, USA (Navy, Marine Corps).

Deployment: Developed by McDonnell aircraft with Northrop collaboration from the latter company's land-based YF-17, the F/A-18A Hornet has had a development process that at times has teetered on the brink of collapse. Intended as a cheap lightweight alternative to the F-14 Tomcat, it predictably matured as an even more costly aircraft; in 1982 the US Navy

Above: The one significant advantage of F/A-18A over F-16 is ability to fire the Sparrow radar-guided medium-range AAM.

Secretary said the unit cost ($24.1m at 1981 prices) was too expensive, and threatened to cancel at the 240th aircraft at the end of Fiscal year 1983. Despite this, the F/A-18 has finally emerged as an aircraft of very useful capability and versatility, which because of its deliberate design to fly both fighter and attack missions with equal effectiveness has won two hard-fought procurement battles in Canada and Spain. Though the US Navy calculates it would be cheaper to build more F-14s and A-6s—in other words to replace their replacement by the original types—this would appear a retrograde move and there is no way such nations as Canada and Spain would consider following suit.

Of course, the F/A-18A is wholly modern in aerodynamics, structure, ▶

Below left: The third development Hornet pictured over a Navy carrier (apparently CVA-68 *Nimitz*) over the Pacific in 1981.

Below: Another view of No 3 prototype, during early carrier trials. In both pictures it has the dogtooth leading edge.

▶ systems, avionics and propulsion, the only old part being the weapons such as the M61, Sparrow and basic Sidewinder. Though not a large aircraft, with dimensions between those of the compact Tornado and the F-4, and significantly smaller than the F-15, the F/A-18 combines the Tornado's advantages of small afterburning engines and large internal fuel capacity with avionics and weapons configured from the start for both F and A missions (hence the unusual designation). Of course, in the low-level attack role it cannot equal Tornado because it has a large wide-span fixed wing, giving severe gust response, and suffers from relatively low maximum speed and lack of terrain-following radar; but in the typical Navy/Marines scenario with a mission mainly over the sea and a dive on target these shortcomings are less important. In weapon carriage the Hornet is first-class, with plenty of pylons and payload capability, and clearance for a wide spectrum of stores. In the fighter mission it is excellent, now that the wing has been redesigned to meet the specified rates of roll, and unlike its most immediate rival, the F-16, has from the start carried a high-power liquid-cooled radar, the Hughes APG-65, matched with radar-guided AAMs: initially Sparrows, notably AIM-7M, to be followed by Amraam when that weapon is developed. This AAM capability played a major part in the selection of the Hornet by foreign customers. Canada's 1st CAG flies primarily in the strike mission, but the CF-18, in which Canadian industry shares, is initially replacing the outdated CF-101 Voodoo in the home air defence role. A total of 137 is being procured, and from 1983 these are to

replace the Voodoo in squadrons 409, 410, 416 and 425 at Comox BC, Bagotville Que and Chatham NB. Only later will the CF-18 replace the CF-104 in No 1 CAG at Baden-Soellingen, Germany. Spain's procurement, as announced in July 1982, is 84 aircraft priced at a hoped-for $3 billion (unit price with spares $35.7 million. Deliveries are due in 1986-92 and Spanish industry was negotiating offset participation as this book went to press. The immediate task with Spain's EdA is to replace the Mirage IIIEE in Esc 111 and 112 but with 84 aircraft it is planned to form four 18-aircraft squadrons. It will be cheaper to leave carrier equipment on the export Hornets, and both foreign customers have signed for a number of two-seat TF/A-18s, which have about 6 per cent less fuel but retain combat capability almost unchanged.

To sum up, the Hornet is probably the best that designers have yet achieved in creating a true multimission combat aircraft. Good avionics and cockpit displays enable one man to fly a whole spectrum of missions—which will expand further if development is completed of a recon nose package which replaces the gun—without excessive workload. Its chief remaining difficulties stem from the effects of inflation which have eroded its planned cost advantages over the F-14.

Below: Mk 83 bombs drop cleanly from the No 4 aircraft during level separation trials in 1979. On a combat mission some pylons would be occupied by tanks, sensors and ECM pods.

Northrop F-5

F-5A Freedom Fighter, F-5B, F-5E Tiger II, F-5F

Origin: Northrop Corporation, USA, with licence assembly in Turkey; early models licensed to Canada and Netherlands.

Type: Light tactical fighter and attack/recon.

Engines: Two General Electric J85 afterburning turbojets, (A/B) 4,080lb (1,850kg) thrust J85-113 or -13A, (E/F) 5,000lb (2,270kg) thrust -21A.

Dimensions: Span (A/B) 25ft 3in (7.7m) (A/B over tip tanks) 25ft 10in (7.87m), (E/F) 26ft 8in (8.13m), (E/F over AAMs) 27ft 11in (8.53m) length (A) 47ft 2in (14.38m), (B) 46ft 4in (14.12m), (E) 48ft 2in (14.68m), (F) 51ft 7in (15.72m); wing area (A/B) 170sq ft (15.79m²), (E/F) 186sq ft (17.3m²).

Weights: Empty (A) 8,085lb (3,667kg), (B) 8,361lb (73,792kg), (E) 9,683lb (4,392kg), (F) 10,567lb (4,793kg); max loaded (A) 20,576lb (9,333kg), (B) 20,116lb (9,124kg), (E) 24,676lb (11,193kg), (F) 25,225lb (11,442kg).

Performance: Maximum speed at 36,000ft (11km), (A) 925mph (1,489km/h, Mach 1.4), (B) 886mph (1,425km/h, Mach 1.34), (E) 1,077mph (1,734km/h, Mach 1.63), (F) 1,011mph (1,628km/h, Mach 1.53); typical cruising speed 562mph (904km/h, Mach 0.85); initial climb (A/B) 28,700ft (8,750m)/min, (E) 34,500ft (10,516m)/min, (F) 32,890ft (1,025m)/min, service ceiling (all) about 51,000ft (15.54km), combat radius with max weapon load and allowances, (A, hi-lo-hi) 215 miles (346km), (E,lo-lo-lo) 138 miles (222km); range with max fuel (all hi, tanks dropped, with reserves) (A) 1,565 miles (2,518km), (E) 1,779 miles (2,863km).

Armament: (A/B) military load 6,200lb (2,812kg) including two 20mm M-39 guns and wide variety of underwing stores, plus AIM-9 AAMs for air combat; (E/F) wide range of ordnance to total of 7,000lb (3,175kg) not including two (F-5F, one) M-39A2 guns each with 280 rounds and two AIM-9 missiles on tip rails.

History: First flight (N-156C) 30 July 1959, (production F-5A) October 1963, (F-5E) 11 August 1972.

Users: Canada, Greece, Netherlands, Norway, Spain, Turkey, USA (AF, Navy).

Deployment: The Northrop N-156F lightweight fighter began to crystallize in 1956, and eventually the first USAF T-38 Talon prototype trainer flew in April 1959 followed by the N-156C fighter in July. At that time nobody had bought the fighter but eventually, with Department of Defense backing, Northrop sold more than 1,040 of the F-5A and two-seat F-5B type, plus a further 115 CF-5s built by Canadair, 102 jointly by Canadair and Fokker for the Netherlands and 70 built by CASA in Spain. All these first-generation F-5s were of basically the same models, the F-5A single-seater and F-5B two-seater, though there were many variations: Norway specified rocket ATO units and airfield arrester hooks, the Canadian CF-5s have more powerful J85 engines (4,300lb/1,950kg) and the Netherlands NF-5s have manoeuvre flaps and larger drop tanks. Large numbers of these relatively simple machines continue in service, mainly in the day attack role with limited air-combat capability provided by two M-39 20mm guns and two Sidewinders. Greece has three squadrons, the Netherlands three squad- ▶

Above: This F-5E is one of ten passed to the US Navy and assigned to the Navy Fighter Weapons School at NAS Miramar, California, for use in 'Aggressor'-type dissimilar air-combat training.

Above: Takeoff, probably from Nellis, of one of the Aggressor F-5Es used by the US Air Force. Together with similar aircraft of the Navy they have been used to evaluate at least 14 colour schemes to reduce air-combat visibility or to confuse the enemy as to attitude.

Left: One of the earlier F-5A generation, serving with the Greek 341 Mira, 111 Pterix, based at Achialos in 1971.

▶ rons (to be replaced by F-16s in 1985-89), Norway two squadrons (being replaced by F-16s now), Spain two squadrons (including SRF-5A recon aircraft) and Turkey five squadrons plus one of RFs.

Canada's CF-5s are being withdrawn and some have been sold to Venezuela. The F-5E and two-seat F-5F Tiger II aircraft have many refinements, notably including a simple Emerson APQ-153 radar and more powerful J85 engines, and though they still do not pretend to be all-weather or sophisticated tactical aircraft they are very attractive because of their low price. By late 1982 the Tiger II had sold to 19 air forces to a total of almost 1,400 additional aircraft. The only NATO customer is the USA itself (not a serious user of the F-5A/B) which has adopted the Tiger II as an economical mount for advanced fighter pilot training. The USAF received 66 for use by Aggressors units, notably for Red Flag training at Nellis and dissimilar air-combat training by the 527th TFS at Alconbury; the Navy has 10 Es and three Fs in Top Gun training at NAS Miramar.

Right: Four of the Aggressors in experimental or simulated Warsaw Pact camouflage, with 'enemy' aircraft nose numbers.

Below: Low-visibility camouflage by a 'Top Gun' F-5E from NAS Miramar is spoilt by red turbine warning bands.

Left: The Netherlands KLu (air force) still uses NF-5A and (as here) two-seat NF-5B Freedom Fighters built in a partnership between Dutch industry and Canadair. This NF-5B was assigned to Nr 313 Squadron at Twenthe and is shown with 'Coke-bottle' wingtip tanks of early F-5s supplemented by a drop tank.

Panavia Tornado ADV

Tornado F.2

Origin: Panavia Aircraft GmbH, with especial responsibility (and assembly and flight test) by British Aerospace.

Type: Two-seat long-range interceptor.

Engines: Two Turbo-Union RB.199 Mk 103 each rated at 16,000lb (7,258kg) thrust with maximum afterburner.

Dimensions: Span (25°) 45ft 7¼in (13.9m), (65°) 28ft 2½in (8.6m); length 59ft 3in (18.06m); height 18ft 8½in (5.7m); wing area not published.

Weights: Empty, equipped, about 31,500lb (14,290kg); takeoff weight (clean, max internal fuel) 47,500lb (21,546kg); maximum not published.

Performance: Maximum speed (clean, at height) about 1,500mph (2,414km/h,Mach 2.27); combat mission with max AAM load, 2h 20min on station at distance of 375 miles (602km) from base with allowance for combat.

Armament: One 27mm Mauser cannon, four Sky Flash (later Amraam) recessed under fuselage and two AIM-9L Sidewinder AAMs (later Asraam).

History: First flight 27 October 1979; service delivery late 1983; operational squadron late 1984.

User: UK (RAF).

Deployment: Development of Tornado ADV (Air-Defence Variant) was authorised by the British Government in March 1976 to provide a replacement for the Lightning and subsequently the Phantom in the RAF air-defence role. None of Britain's NATO partners has to defend so large a volume of airspace, extending from Iceland to the Dutch coast and from the Atlantic approaches to the Baltic. The task demands an aircraft possessed not only of very high performance but also very long range (at lowest fuel cost), the most modern long-range radar, and missiles with snap-down capability against intruders at very low altitude, and the ability to operate autonomously at great distances from any friendly base in the worst ▶

134

Above: Despite its optically flat windscreen and large two-man canopy the Tornado F.2 is the world's fastest aircraft at low level, and one of the fastest at higher altitudes.

Below: First ADV prototype flew in October 1979. This version is tailored to RAF requirements, but there would be no problem in producing a multi-role interceptor/attack variant.

▶ possible weather, at night, against multiple targets, at all altitudes, in the most severe ECM conditions. The task is wholly beyond the capacity of the Lightning, and even the Phantom cannot meet any of these demands fully. In contrast, the Tornado provided a basis for what is certainly the best and most cost/effective long-range interceptor in the Western world. Much of the basic aircraft, especially including the German centre fuselage and Italian wings, remains almost unchanged from the three-nation IDS version. The forward fuselage, made by BAe, is new. To accommodate the four medium-range missiles (initially Sky Flash) recessed under the belly the overall length is increased by 53½in (1.36m), which in turn increases internal fuel by 200gal (909litres). The inflight-refuelling probe is a permanent retractable installation on the left of the cockpit instead of a detachable unit on the right. The main radar is the completely new Marconi/Ferranti Foxhunter pulse-doppler set with track-while-scan capability, in a longer and more pointed radome which improves supersonic acceleration. Extremely comprehensive communications and IFF equipment is carried, plus a low-light TV for greatly magnified visual image ranges in the 100-mile (161km) region. The fixed wing nibs are larger, more swept, and devoid of Krüger flaps. Flight trials proved outstandingly successful, and from 1984 Tornado F.2s will replace Lightnings in 5 and 11 Sqns followed by the Phantoms of 23, 29, 43, 56 and 111 Sqns. A total of 165 is required, in addition to the three prototypes, and 70 were on order in 1982 (18 in the fourth Tornado production batch of 162 aircraft, and 52 in the fifth batch of 171); a further increment was due in early 1983 bringing the total by that year close to the RAF requirement. It is considered highly likely that other NATO countries will also purchase this aircraft.

Right: Fuselage of the interceptor was lengthened in order to accommodate tandem pairs of Sky Flash missiles. This enabled an additional 200gal (909 litres) of fuel to be accommodated and, with reduced nose angle, has improved speed and acceleration.

Below right: The first prototype in a tight turn with wings at their maximum 68° angle. With two tanks, as here, a CAP endurance of 4h 13min without refuelling has been demonstrated.

Below: An unusual attitude by a later Tornado F.2: steep climb with gear down and engines in cold thrust. Note the full-span double-slotted flaps and (just visible) leading-edge slats.

137

Panavia Tornado IDS

Tornado IDS (GR.1) and dual (T.3)

Origin: Panavia Aircraft GmbH, international company formed by British Aerospace, MBB of W. Germany and Aeritalia.

Type: Two-seat multi-role combat aircraft optimised for strike, (T) dual trainer.

Engines: Two Turbo-Union RB.199 Mk 101 or 103 augmented turbofans each rated at 15,800lb (7,167kg) with full afterburner.

Dimensions: Span (25°) 45ft 7¼in (13.90m), (65°) 28ft 2½in (8.60m); length 54ft 9½in (16.7m), height 18ft 8½in (5.7m); wing area not published.

Weights: Empty, equipped, about 30,865lb (14,000kg); loaded (clean) about 45,000lb (20,411kg); maximum loaded, about 60,000lb (18,150kg).

Performance: Maximum speed (clean), at sea level, over 920mph (1,480km/h, Mach 1.2), at height, over 1,452mph (2,337km/h, Mach 2.2); service ceiling over 50,000ft (15,240m); combat radius (8,000lb/3,629kg bombs, hi-lo-hi) 863 miles (1,390km).

Armament: Two 27mm Mauser cannon in lower forward fuselage; seven pylons, three tandem on body and four on the swinging wings, for external load up to 18,000lb (8,165kg).

History: First flight (prototype) 14 August 1974, (production IDS) July 1979; service delivery (IDS to trials unit) February 1978, (squadron service, RAF, Luft, MFG) 1982.

Users: W Germany (Luftwaffe, Marineflieger), Italy, UK (RAF). ▶

Above: A 1975 picture of the third prototype carrying ECM pods, tanks and eight dummy bombs of low-drag 1,000lb (Mk 83) type.

Above: Another view of the same aircraft in the same loaded configuration as seen at left. The production ECM pod for the RAF Tornado force is at present the MSDS ARI.23246/1, sometimes known as Sky Shadow (and originally as Ajax).

Below: Tail number G-24 means 24th Luftwaffe single-seater, and TTTE tail badge means the Trinational Tornado Training Establishment.

Above: It is possible to take off in cold thrust, and this MFG aircraft is doing just that; location is TTTE at Cottesmore.

▶ **Deployment:** With the F-16 the Tornado is the most important aircraft in the NATO alliance in Europe. Unlike all other aircraft it was designed specifically to meet the requirements of four major customers in three nations, and it is remarkable that three nations working in partnership should have succeeded in creating an aircraft at once so outstanding in capability and versatility and so uniform in its first four customer variants (the RAF interceptor variant is described separately). Its baseline missions are similar to those of the F-111, but the Tornado differs in being more compact, lighter and much more fuel-efficient, and in having avionics ten years later in conception. The most experienced attack crews are unanimous in claiming that it is the first aircraft in history which can be flown on long missions at night or in bad weather at treetop height without severe strain, tiredness or any degradation in human performance.

Features include an advanced multimode forward-looking radar with the option of various types of programmable software, a TFR (terrain-following radar), electrically signalled FBW (fly-by-wire) flight controls with artificial stability, fully variable supersonic inlets (which help make this the fastest aircraft in the world at low level, and one of the fastest at all heights, despite the extremely compact lightweight engines), advanced avionic systems to manage the array of stores which can be carried (which exceeds that of any other aircraft) and modern tandem cockpits with head-up and head-down displays in the front and three electronic displays in the back. Among the stores which had been cleared by 1983 are all tactical bombs of the four initial customers, nine rocket pods, Sidewinder AAMs and Sea Eagle, Kormoran, Maverick, Hobos, Paveway, AS.30 and AS.30L, Martel (seldom to be carried), Aspide, BL.755, JP.233 and MW-1; Harpoon and possibly ▶

Above: Three aircraft—two RAF and one Luftwaffe—on a training sortie from the TTTE at Cottesmore seen in early 1981.

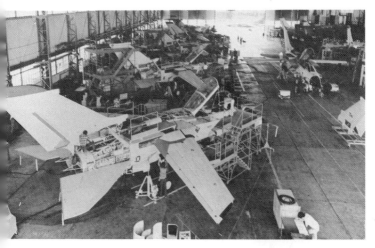

Above: Eight Tornados being assembled at Aeritalia's Turin, Caselle, plant, out of 100 on order for AMI.

Left: This Tornado was built as the 04 prototype, flown in 1975 as D-9592, and later repainted as shown in MFG markings for testing at the Erpröbungsstelle 61 at Manching, Germany. Note four Kormoran missiles.

▶ MRASM will also be cleared later. All versions have comprehensive internal radar warning systems, and while German and Italian Tornados carry the EL/73 deception jammer (developed by Elettronica, AEG-Telefunken and MSDS) the RAF aircraft use the ARI.23246 (Sky Shadow) by MSDS with parts by BAe, Plessey and Racal-Decca.

Deliveries began to the TTTE (Tornado Tri-national Training Establishment) at RAF Cottesmore in 1980, which had its complement of 50 aircraft in 1982. By the latter year the RAF weapon training unit at Honington was in full operation as was the Luftwaffe equivalent at Erding, and RAF No 9 (IX) Sqn had converted from Vulcans and Marineflieger MFG 1 had largely converted from the F-104G. Deliveries by late 1982 were close to 150, despite a slow-down in planned rate of deliveries. Including four of the six pre-series aircraft, but none of the nine prototypes, the total procurement of the IDS (interdiction strike) version for the four original customers is 644: 220 Tornado GR.1 for the RAF, 212 for the Luftwaffe, 112 for the Marineflieger and 100 for the Italian AMI. By late 1982 contracts had been signed for five production batches: 40 (20 GR.1 for the RAF, 17 for the Luftwaffe/Marineflieger and three prototype ADVs; 110 (55 RAF, 40 Luftwaffe/Marineflieger and 15 AMI); 164 (68 RAF, 68 Luftwaffe/Marineflieger and 28 AMI); 162 (53 RAF plus 18 production F.2 included); and 171 (52 F.2), making a total at that time of 647.

The RAF GR.1s replace the Vulcan in the long-range interdiction role, normally operating from UK airfields (the first to convert, No IX, is based at Honington, the unit previously having been at Waddington). It has not been announced how many GR.1 squadrons will be based in the UK (presumably all in 1 Group) nor whether a dedicated multisensor Tornado variant will replace the Vulcan SR.2s of 27 Sqn in the maritime reconnaissance role. In RAF Germany (2 ATAF) the GR.1 is progressively replacing the Jaguar in the three-squadron strike wing at Brüggen, and four squadrons will replace the two Buccaneer units at Laarbruch and the Jaguar recon squadron. This in effect adds one squadron (eight replacing seven) and implies a multisensor Tornado, probably a standard aircraft carrying the advanced IR system being developed by BAe Dynamics, plus optical cameras.

Above: One of the German-assembled prototypes (believed to be No 07, which introduced an almost complete internal avionic kit) parked at Manching with fuselage bombs, tanks, ECM, data-link and instrumentation pods. Cover plates are fitted in the inlets.

Below: The 13th Tornado, first with production kinked taileron, was used for flight testing the bulky, high-drag MW-1 dispenser which comprises four sections each with 28 double-ended tubes from which bomblets or delay-action mines are projected.

Rockwell International B-1

B-1B

Origin: Rockwell International, North American Aerospace Operations, USA.

Type: Strategic bomber and missile platform.

Engines: Four General Electric F101-GE-102 augmented turbofans each rated at 29,900lb (13,563kg) with full afterburner.

Dimensions: Span (fully spread) 136ft 8½in (41.67m), (fully swept, to 67.5°) 78ft 2½in (23.84m); length (including probe) 150ft 2½in (45.78m); wing area (spread, gross) 1,950sq ft (181.2m²).

Weights: Empty about 160,000lb (72,576kg); maximum loaded 477,000lb (216,367kg).

Performance: Maximum speed (over 36,000ft/11km) about 1,000mph (1,600km/h, Mach 1.5), (500ft/152m) 750mph (1,205km/h, Mach 0.99); typical high-altitude cruising speed, 620mph (1,000km/h); range with maximum internal fuel, over 7,000 miles (11,265km); field length, less than 4,500ft (1,372m).

Armament: Eight ALCM internal in weapon bays separated by movable bulkhead, plus 14 external; 24 SRAM internal plus 14 external; 12 B28 or B43 internal plus 8/14 external; 24 B61 or B83 internal plus 14 external; 84 Mk 82 internal plus 44 external (80,000lb, 36,288kg).

History: Original (AMSA) study 1962; contracts for engine and airframe 5 June 1970; first flight 23 December 1974; decision against production June 1977; termination of flight-test programme 30 April 1981; announcement of intention to produce for inventory, September 1981; first flight March 1985; first delivery, late 1985; planned IOC, 1 July 1987.

User: USA (Air Force). ▶

Below: The No 4 prototype has the dorsal spine, blunt tail and many other external features which will be repeated on the B-1B.

Above: Like the basic aircraft the cockpit has developed greatly since the 'Hi-Fi' mockup of 1971; B-1B will have small changes.

▶ **Deployment:** No aircraft in history has had so long a gestation as the B-1 strategic bomber, planned since 1962 under different names and configurations as a replacement for the B-52. Eventually four B-1A prototypes were tested, but in June 1977 President Carter cancelled the programme. It was resurrected in September 1981 when President Reagan announced that 100 of an improved model, the B-1B, would at last be built for Strategic Air Command. Development is being helped by resuming flight testing of B-1A Nos 2 and 4, and externally these (especially No 4) look very like a B-1B. Features of the latter will include total concentration on low-level subsonic operations, with fixed engine inlets and conventional ejection seats instead of a crew capsule, and flexibility to carry conventional bombs and various ASMs as well as nuclear free-fall bombs. The B-1B dispenses with further high-altitude dash features, the wing sweep being reduced to about 59.5°. As well as refined engines the B-1B can carry much more fuel, a detailed weight-reduction programme reduces empty weight, while gross weight is raised by over 37 tonnes. Main gears are stronger, wing gloves and engine inlets totally redesigned, many parts (ride-control fins, flaps and bomb doors, for example) made of composite material, pneumatic starters with cross-bleed fitted, offensive avionics completely updated (main radar is Westinghouse's APG-66), the ALQ-161 defensive avionics subsystem fitted, RAM (radar-absorbent material) fitted at some 85 locations throughout the airframe, and the whole aircraft nuclear-hardened and given Multiplex wiring.

Radar cross-section will be less than one-hundredth that of a B-52 (and only one-tenth that of a B-1A) at 10sq ft (0.93m^2), and the avionic systems will be dramatically more capable even than those of the B-1A which were revolutionary for their period. A classified study showed that even the B-1A would have remarkable capability to penetrate large and heavily defended regions of airspace, and the B-1B is expected to be a viable weapon until at least 2000 (the US Defense Secretary caused a stormy reaction from everyone associated with the B-1B when he said it would "penetrate Soviet airspace only until 1989 or 1990"; all evidence shows this to be a surprising misconception, possibly in order to increase political acceptance of the proposed next-generation 'stealth' bomber). B-1B programme cost has been estimated at $20.5 to $39 billion, in 1981 dollars, and the main argument now is whether it might not be better to wait for the 'stealth' aircraft. To do so would be an extremely foolish choice.

Above: Tail-on aspect of fourth aircraft, showing blunt tail with vortex generators. Subcontractor for the two rear-fuselage sections is Vought, much of the skin being titanium alloy.

Below left: Radar cross-section of the four B-1A prototypes has averaged about one-tenth that of a B-52 from frontal aspects. Production B-1B is expected to be roughly ten times better still.

Below: The long-span flaps are visible on the unswept wings in this takeoff picture. There are no ailerons, and the production bomber will have simplified lower-drag overwing root fairings.

Rockwell International OV-10 Bronco

OV-10A to -10E

Origin: Rockwell International, USA.

Type: (Except B) two-seat multi-role counter-insurgency; (B) target tug.

Engines: (Except B(Z)) two 715ehp Garrett T76-410/411 turboprops; (B(Z)) as other versions plus General Electric J85-4 turbojet of 2,950lb (1,338kg) thrust above fuselage.

Dimensions: Span 40ft (12.19m); length (except D) 41ft 7in (12.67m), (D) 44ft (13.4m); height 15ft 2in (4.62m); wing area 291sq ft (27.03m²).

Weights: Empty (A) 6,969lb (3,161kg); maximum loaded (A) 14,466lb (6,563kg).

Performance: Maximum speed (A, sea level, clean) 281 mph (452km/h); initial climb 2,300ft (700m)/min; (B(Z)) 6,800ft/min; service ceiling 30,000ft (9,150m); range with maximum weapon load, about 600 miles (960km); ferry range at 12,000lb gross, 1,428 miles (2,300km).

Armament: Four 7.62mm M60C machine guns in sponsons; 1,200lb (544kg) hardpoint on centreline and four 600lb (272kg) points under sponsons; one Sidewinder missile rail under each wing; (OV-10D) as other versions plus three-barrel 20mm cannon in remotely aimed ventral power turret.

History: First flight 16 July 1965; (production OV-10A) 6 August 1967; (YOV-10D) 9 June 1970.

Users: W Germany, USA (Air Force, Marine Corps).

Deployment: Sole outcome of the prolonged studies of CoIn (counter-insurgency) aircraft in the USA in the early 1960s, the OV-10 is a unique aircraft which combines STOL rough-field capability, inflight agility, protection against small-arms fire at low levels, a wide spread of tactical weapons and a nacelle seating pilot and observer in tandem (with an almost perfect view) with a cabin behind for cargo including five paratroops or two stretcher (litter) casualties. These eager machines hum and buzz in

Above: This Marine Corps YOV-10D prototype has now led to squadron deployment of 17 basically similar OV-10D Night Observation Surveillance aircraft with much new equipment.

many parts of the world, including Federal Germany where the Luftwaffe uses six OV-10Bs and 12 OV-10B(Z)s for target-towing duties. The USAF received 157 OV-10As used in the FAC (forward air control) role, and these now serve in the utility role as well as practising the light armed recon and attack mission. One of several units using the type is the 4th ATAF: the 601st TCW at Sembach AB, Germany. The US Marine Corps has 24 OV-10Ds with greatly augmented avionics deployed in three squadrons in the NOS (night observation surveillance) role.

Below: Rocket practice with an OV-10A of the US Air Force.

Saab 35 Draken

J35D and F, Sk35C, S35E and export versions

Origin: Saab-Scania AB, Sweden.

Type: (J35, F-35) single-seat all-weather fighter-bomber; (Sk35, TF-35) dual trainer; (S35) single-seat all-weather reconnaissance.

Engine: One Svenska Flygmotor RM6 (licence-built Rolls-Royce Avon with SFA afterburner): (D, E, F and export) 17,110lb (7,761kg) RM6C.

Dimensions: Span 30ft 10in (9.4m); length 50ft 4in (15.4m) (S35E, 52ft, 15.8m); height 12ft 9in (3.9m); wing area 529.6sq ft (49.2m²).

Weights: Empty (D) 16,017lb; (F) 18,180lb (8,250kg); maximum loaded (D) 22,663lb (10,280kg); (F) 27,050lb (12,270kg); (F-35) 35,275lb (16,000kg).

Performance: Maximum speed (D onwards, clean) 1,320mph (2,125km/h, Mach 2.0), (with two drop tanks and two 1,000lb bombs) 924mph (1,487km/h, Mach 1.4); initial climb (D onwards, clean) 34,450ft (10,500m)/min; service ceiling (D onwards, clean) about 65,000ft (20,000m); range (internal fuel plus external weapons, typical) 800 miles (1,300km), (maximum fuel) 2,020 miles (3,250km).

Armament: (F) one 30mm Aden plus two RB27 Falcon (radar) and two RB28 Falcon (infra-red) missiles, plus two or four RB24; (F-35) two 30mm Aden plus nine stores pylons each rated at 1,000lb (454kg) all usable simultaneously, plus four RB24.

History: First flight 25 October 1955; (production J35A) 15 February 1958; final delivery (35XS) 1975, (Danish TF-35) 1976.
User: Denmark.

Deployment: This highly supersonic aircraft was by far the most advanced warplane on the drawing boards of Western Europe in the early 1950s, and when the first production version entered service in Sweden in 1959 it essentially did the same job as the Lightning with just one afterburning Avon instead of two, and with greater range. In NATO the Draken is flown by the Danish KDF, which has rapidly replaced its F-100s and F-104s by the F-16 but will keep the popular Drakens at least until 1987. They equip the Karup wing, comprising 725 Esk (squadron) tasked in the ground attack role and 729 in the reconnaissance role, in each case with 17 or 18 single-seaters backed up by two-seat TF-35s. The F-35s of No 725 are being completely overhauled and refurbished with a structural audit to give an extended life in high-speed missions at low level with heavy bombloads, and new avionics including an advanced HUD (head-up display) and weapon-delivery systems. The Drakens combine short field-length, excellent manoeuvrability at all heights, good serviceability at low cost and the ability to give a good account of themselves in the secondary air-combat role with guns and Sidewinders.

Below: One of the last Draken variants was the Danish TF-35, a multirole combat-capable tandem-seater usually used for training.

SEPECAT Jaguar

Jaguar GR.1 and T.2, Jaguar A and E

Origin: SEPECAT, consortium formed by British Aerospace (BAC) and Dassault-Breguet, France.

Type: (GR.1 and A) single-seat all-weather attack; (T.2 and E) dual operational trainer.

Engines: Two Rolls-Royce/Turboméca Adour augmented turbofans: (A, E) 7,305lb (3,313kg) Adour 102; (GR.1, T.2) 8,040lb (3,647kg) Adour 104.

Dimensions: Span 28ft 6in (8.69m); length (except T.2, E) 50ft 11in (15.52m); (T.2, E) 53ft 11in (16.42m); height 16ft 0½in (4.89m); wing area 260.27sq ft (24.18m²).

Weights: Empty, about 15,432lb (7,000kg); "normal take-off" (internal fuel and gun ammunition) 24,149lb (10,954kg); maximum loaded 34,612lb (15,700kg).

Performance: Maximum speed (lo, some external stores) 840mph (1,350km/h, Mach 1.1), (hi, some external stores) 1,055mph (1,700km/h, Mach 1.6); attack radius, no external fuel, hi-lo-hi with bombs, 530 miles (852km); ferry range 2,614 miles (4,210km).

Armament: (A, E) two 30mm DEFA 553 each with 150 rounds; five pylons for total external load of 10,500lb (4,763kg); GR.1 as above but guns two 30mm Aden; (T.2) as above but single Aden.

History: First flight (E) 8 September 1968; (production E) 2 November 1971; (production GR.1) 11 October 1972; squadron delivery (E, A) May 1972, (GR, T) June 1973.

Users: France, UK (RAF).

Deployment: Developed jointly by BAC (now BAe) in Britain and Dassault-Breguet in France, to meet a joint requirement of the Armée de l'Air and RAF, the Jaguar matured as an extremely capable and useful tactical attack aircraft, with a combat-capable two-seat version used mainly as an advanced and weapons trainer, the extra seat displacing the nose avionics and leaving fuel capacity unchanged. Powered by two very small afterburning turbofans, the Jaguar stands high off the ground on landing gears with levered-suspension and twin wheels, making the aircraft eminently ▶

Above: Jaguar A of l'Armée de l'air which is clean except for the 264gal (1200 litre) drop tank. France wants updated Jaguars throughout the 1980s.

Below: Armée de l'Air EC4/11 'Jura' has late A-type Jaguars (this is A121) with Atlis II laser guidance, though this cannot guide these 'iron bombs'.

▶ suitable for off-base dispersal even with very heavy external weapons loads—a capability foolishly seldom practised, so that even these aircraft could at any time be caught on their airfields. RAF Germany has a complete wing at Brüggen tasked in the army support and strike role (17, 20 and 31 Sqns) and at Laarbruch is a combined strike and reconnaissance unit using a multisensor external pod (2, written II, Sqn). The RAF aircraft have comprehensive inertial nav/attack systems with a chisel-nose laser and adequate equipment for one-man weapon delivery in adverse conditions. Normal weapons carried are 1,000lb (454kg) or nuclear bombs, rockets and BL.755 cluster dispensers. This wing will progressively be re-equipped with the Tornado GR.1. A further three squadrons (6, 41 and 54) are based at RAF Coltishall, Norfolk, tasked with army support and with No 41 also having the recon pods. All RAF Jaguars have uprated Mk 104 engines. ECM includes the usual fin-mounted ARI.18223 passive warning, but perhaps shortsightedly it has been decided to abandon long-discussed plans to fit internal active countermeasures, just as it has been decided to drop the idea of fitting larger high-lift supercritical wings.

France received the last of its 200 Jaguars in December 1981. These retain the original Mk 102 engine and have a twin-gyro platform and doppler instead of an inertial system, no laser and seats which cannot be used at below 104mph (167km/h). A mix of A and E aircraft equips three squadrons of EC 3 at Nancy, three of EC 7 at St Dizier with a fourth in the nuclear role at Istres, three of EC 11 at Toul/Rosières and EC 4/11 at Bordeaux. The newest 30 Jaguar As have an Atlis II (laser/TV) pod used in conjunction with the AS.30L smart missile. The Armée de l'Air has several update proposals for its Jaguars, which are expected to remain in use until at least 1989.

Above: A rare echelon of GR.1 single-seaters from all five RAF Germany squadrons; No 2 (foreground) carries the recon pod.

Below: Vapour streams from the wingtips of two Jaguar GR.1s of RAF No 20 Sqn, from Brüggen, as they pull round a *schloss* waypoint.

Vought A-7 Corsair II

A-7A to A-7P

Origin: Vought Corporation, USA.

Type: (except K) attack, (K) combat trainer.

Engine: (D, H, K) one 14,250lb (6,465kg) thrust Allison TF41-1 turbofan; (E) one 15,000lb (6,804kg) TF41-2; (P) one 12,200lb (5,534kg) Pratt & Whitney TF30-408 turbofan.

Dimensions: Span 38ft 9in (11.8m); length (D) 46ft 1½in (14.06m), (K) 48ft 11½in (14.92m); wing area 375sq ft (34.83m).

Weights: Empty (D) 19,781lb (8,972kg), loaded (D) 42,000lb (19,050kg).

Performance: Maximum speed (D, clean, SL), 690mph (1,110km/h) (5,000ft/1,525m, with 12 Mk 82 bombs) 646mph (1,040km/h); tactical radius (with unspecified weapon load at unspecified height), 715 miles (1,151km); ferry range (internal fuel) 2,281 miles (3,671km), (max with external tanks) 2,861 miles (4,604km).

Armament: One 20mm M61A-1 gun with 1,000 rounds, and up to 15,000lb (6,804kg) of tactical weapons on eight hardpoints (two on fuselage each rated 500lb/227kg, two inboard wing pylons each 2,500lb/1,134kg, four outboard wing pylons each 3,500lb/1,587kg).

History: First flight (Navy A-7A) 27 September 1965, (D) 26 September 1968 (K) January 1981.

Users: Greece, Portugal, USA (Navy, ANG).

Deployment: The Corsair II was originally derived from the supersonic F-8 Crusader fighter to meet a Navy need for a subsonic tactical attack aircraft with a much heavier bomb load and greater fuel capacity than the A-4. So effective did the A-7 prove that in 1966 it was selected to equip a substantial proportion of USAF TAC wings, and ultimately 457 A-7Ds were acquired. These introduced a more powerful engine (derived from the Rolls-Royce Spey) with gas-turbine self-starting, and multi-barrel gun, and a totally revised avionic system for continuous solution of navigation problems and precision placement of free-fall weapons in all weather. The folding wings and arrester hook were retained and other features included a strike camera, boom receptacle instead of a probe, boron carbide armour over cockpit and engine, and a McDonnell Douglas Escapac seat. Avionics have been further improved over the years, but the main features of all Corsair IIs have always been a robust airframe and systems, good range and endurance, the ability to carry heavy and varied loads, and air/ground delivery accuracy which set a new standard that has only recently been surpassed by the F-16 and F/A-18. All the active force of 350 A-7Ds have been passed to the ANG, but in time of crisis any of these could deploy to Europe or other trouble-spots in 48 hours, with in-flight refuelling for the transatlantic crossing. In the Navy the current version is the A-7E, which was based on the USAF A-7D! This still highly effective machine is very much a front-line aircraft, equipping 24 attack squadrons (ashore or embarked) plus two shore-based training squadrons. Of these 13 are ▶

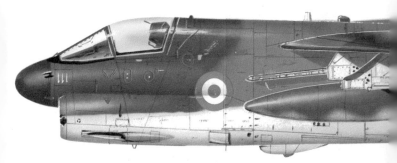

Above: Seen here before delivery from the Vought plant at Dallas, this A-7H serves with the Elliniki Aeroporia (Greek AF), which has three squadrons, Nos 340, 345 and 347. They were bought new.

Above: Final production Corsair was the A-7K, a combat-capable two-seater for the US Air National Guard. This particular K went to the 162nd Tactical Fighter Training Group, Arizona ANG.

Below: The A-7H (H for Hellenic) is the only type of A-7 Corsair II built for export; it retains carrier-compatible features, such as folding wings, to save cost. Portuguese A-7s are ex-USN.

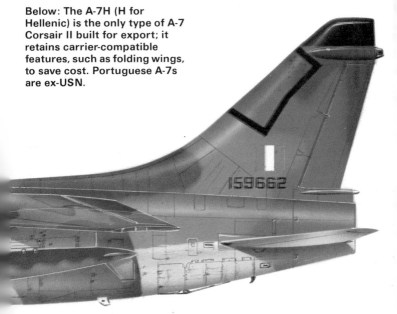

157

assigned to the Atlantic Fleet. A further six Navy Reserve squadrons fly the earlier TF30-powered A-7B. Newest of all the US variants is the two-seat A-7K, 42 of which should by late 1983 have been distributed in pairs to 11 of the 13 ANG combat-ready A-7D units plus a further 16 to the 162nd Tac Fighter Training Group at Tucson. A direct-view tube provides for Walleye and similar TV ASM guidance, and Pave Penny pods are carried for laser-guided stores, but accuracies are in the range 2-3m (say 8ft) with free-fall bombs.

Among European customers, Greece purchased 60 A-7H new from Vought, and these are virtually A-7Es with the more powerful model of TF41, and the pilots trained with the US Navy and not the USAF. The H equips three mira (squadrons), all in the maritime support and anti-ship role: 340

and 345 at Souda Bay, Crete, and 347 at Larissa in the north. The Elliniki Aeroporia also bought six two-seat TA-7H similar to the A-7K. Portugal was eager to obtain more effective combat aircraft but had little money, and eventually selected 20 A-7As well-used by the US Navy and before delivery completely refurbished by Vought. The engine remains the TF30 but improved to P-408 standard, and the avionics have been brought up virtually to A-7E standard. These aircraft equip Esc 302 at Monte Real, replacing the F-86 but tasked primarily in the strike role; the FAP still needs an air-combat fighter.

Below: 500lb (227kg) Snakeye retarded bombs occupy the wing pylons of this A-7D of the 23rd TFW, England AFB, Louisiana.

OTHER SUPER-VALUE MILITARY GUIDES IN THIS SERIES......

OTHER ILLUSTRATED MILITARY GUIDES NOW AVAILABLE..

Allied Fighters of World War II
Bombers of World War II
German, Italian and Japanese Fighters
of World War II
Modern Fighters and
Attack Aircraft
Modern Soviet Navy

Modern Submarines
Modern Tanks
Modern US Navy
Modern Warships
Pistols and Revolvers
Rifles and Sub-Machine Guns
World War II Tanks

* Each has 160 fact-filled pages
* Each is colourfully illustrated with hundreds of action photographs
  and technical drawings
* Each contains concisely presented data and accurate descriptions
  of major international weapons
* Each represents tremendous value

Further titles in this series are in preparation
Your military library will be incomplete without them.

PRINTED IN BELGIUM BY

INTERNATIONAL BOOK PRODUCTION